ESTIMATING THE JOB CREATION IMPACT OF DEVELOPMENT ASSISTANCE

Yesim Elhan-Kayalar and Sothea Oum

DECEMBER 2022

ADB

ASIAN DEVELOPMENT BANK

Corrigenda to ADB publications may be found at http://www.adb.org/publications/corrigenda.

Notes:
In this publication, "$" refers to United States dollars.
ADB recognizes "Vietnam" as Viet Nam.
Some numbers quoted in this publication may not be exact due to rounding.

On the cover: (*top-left*) Workers at Waila Water Treatment Plant in Suva, Fiji; (*right*) Maintenance workers at Vena Energy Solar Farm in Selong, Indonesia; (*bottom-left*) A farmer growing organic vegetables in Khon Kaen, Thailand (ADB Multimedia Library).

Cover design by Rhommel Rico.

Contents

Tables and Figure

Figure

Abbreviations

ADB	Asian Development Bank
BPS	Statistics Indonesia
CGE	computable general equilibrium
COVID-19	coronavirus disease
FTE	full-time equivalent
GDP	gross domestic product
GTAP	Global Trade Analysis Project
IFC	International Finance Corporation
ILO	International Labour Organization
IO	input–output
LFS	labor force survey
MRIOT	multi-regional input–output table
PBL	policy-based lending
TA	technical assistance
UMIC	upper-middle-income country

Summary

The Asian Development Bank (ADB) Corporate Results Framework 2019–2024 sets out indicators to assess the impact and value addition of its operations. In this framework, one measure of operational effectiveness is the number of jobs created as a result of ADB support. A review of selected country portfolios and jobs data for 2010–2019 reveals that the total job creation impact of ADB operations is underreported.

In this study, input–output (IO) and computable general equilibrium (CGE) models are used to develop a customized approach for ADB operations that would improve the fit and predictiveness of jobs impact assessments. In the first phase of this study, a methodology was developed to estimate potential direct, indirect, and induced job creation through ADB project and program portfolios in Fiji, Indonesia, and Thailand during 2010–2019. It used the 2021 ADB multi-regional input–output tables (MRIOTs), national statistics, and data from the International Labour Organization (ILO) and Global Trade Analysis Project (GTAP). These three upper-middle-income countries were selected as pilot cases for this study due to the representative characteristics of their portfolios for the rest of ADB developing members.

In the second phase, model-generated estimates were compared with reported jobs data in operations documents to identify any discrepancies between estimated and reported data, and means to address the discrepancies. Finally, a robustness check was done by applying IO and CGE models to selected projects and programs in different sectors. Findings indicate that the linear, simpler to construct and use IO models may be preferable for projects that support substantial local purchases of non-construction capital goods and services (as compared to imported goods); while the more comprehensive, data-intensive CGE models can help capture the broader-based impact of programmatic policy support and large-scale projects. It is expected that as the model is further tested in selected projects and programs under design or implementation, the fit would further improve. In addition, improving data capture and systematic monitoring can complement quantitative assessments and support poverty reduction impact assessments. The model—with robust data—can be applied to assess and enhance the operational effectiveness of ADB, and to inform government investment decisions and policies to promote inclusive growth.

The authors would like to thank the Economic Research and Regional Cooperation Department (ERCD) Seminar Series participants; ADB's Pacific Subregional Office, Indonesia Resident Mission, and Thailand Resident Mission country directors and staff for their helpful feedback during the seminars and consultations held on this study. Any remaining errors are the authors' responsibility.

Introduction 1

Understanding the impact of development assistance programs and projects can help governments and international development agencies—such as the Asian Development Bank (ADB)—further enhance the effectiveness of their interventions. In ADB, the impact evaluation process is guided by *Cost–Benefit Analysis for Development: A Practical Guide* (ADB 2013a) and *Impact Evaluation of Development Interventions: A Practical Guide* (White and Raitzer 2017), among others. The complementarity between the economic analysis of the former and the impact evaluation of the latter is used to provide evidence-based, effective outcomes, and inform future policy interventions and development assistance to optimize ADB's contributions to the Sustainable Development Goals.

Creating decent jobs for all—in particular for the most vulnerable, underserved, and marginalized population segments—can be an effective poverty reduction tool and foster inclusive growth.[1] This is a priority for many development agencies, including ADB. Job creation is one of the results framework indicators of the *ADB Strategy 2030* (ADB 2018a) and it is included in the *ADB Corporate Results Framework 2019–2024* (ADB 2019).

Job creation has been increasingly used as a measure of operational effectiveness by international development agencies. The International Finance Corporation (IFC) has been reporting private sector contributions to job creation and suggests that the estimates should cover not only direct jobs, but indirect and induced jobs, second-order "growth" effects, and net job creation.[2] The World Bank's *2013 World Development Report* was dedicated to employment and its International Development Association focused on jobs and economic transformation in 2019 (World Bank 2012 and 2019).

ADB has adopted job creation—with added emphasis on skilled jobs for women—as one of the criteria for assessing the value created through its development assistance and the effectiveness of its operations in 2019. In 2019 and 2020, these two results indicators were monitored through available data at project and program completion. This approach entailed summation of direct jobs created—as reported in project and program completion documents in a given year—based on various definitions of employment; data collection; validation criteria; and different combinations

---

[1] According to the *Results Framework Indicator Definitions* (ADB 2020), "Jobs refer to activities that generate income, monetary or in kind, and follow standards of decent work as defined by the International Labour Organization (ILO)." The ILO definition of decent work is "opportunities for women and men to obtain decent and productive work, in conditions of freedom, equity, security and human dignity" (Anker et al. 2002).

[2] "Indirect jobs" are employment changes in suppliers and distributors. "Induced employment" refers to jobs resulting from direct and indirect employees spending more and increasing consumption. "Secondary effects" refer to job creation through benefits of improved access to infrastructure, such as access to more reliable power allowing enterprises to produce more efficiently. "Net job creation" incorporates effects accounting for job losses among competitors (IFC 2013).

of calculations and estimations in its sovereign and nonsovereign operations. ADB's *Development Effectiveness Report* has reflected only direct jobs created since 2019 (ADB 2020a, 2021, 2022). A model that helps estimate the impact of ADB operations in creating direct, indirect, and induced jobs can help provide a more complete assessment and rectify underreporting witnessed. This extended assessment would support ex ante assessment of possible employment impact during project design and the ex post evaluation of possible employment impacts resulting from the project. These findings can also inform future project or program design to improve the effectiveness of future interventions in generating inclusive growth in ADB developing members.

The objective of this report is to review the methodologies that are used by national, bilateral, and multilateral development agencies, and to develop a methodology that can be useful in assessing the impact of ADB sovereign and nonsovereign development interventions (i.e., capital investments, policy-based lending) on job creation. The report aims to develop a practical methodology to estimate direct, indirect, and induced jobs created as a result of ADB sovereign and nonsovereign operations; one that yields robust estimates, can be implemented systematically in all ADB operations, and with analytical requirements optimized to manage additional transaction costs for operations teams.

Three countries (Fiji, Indonesia, Thailand) were selected as pilots to test this methodology, for their common and distinctive characteristics among ADB members. They are all upper-middle-income countries (UMICs), as most ADB members are expected to reach UMIC status by 2030. Fiji is a special UMIC case, as a small, fragile island economy, where most ADB assistance has been in the form of sovereign lending. The majority of ADB operations in Indonesia were sovereign lending, with a significant portion dedicated to budgetary support. ADB operations in Thailand during 2010–2019 comprised predominantly nonsovereign projects. Differences in outcomes and employment impacts of ADB operations in these countries provide insights into job creation through different ADB loan instruments provided to public and private sectors.

Section 2 of this study provides a brief review of methodologies used in employment impact analyses and the methodology proposed to monitor employment outcomes and the effectiveness of ADB operations in creating jobs. Section 3 summarizes the estimates of direct, indirect, and induced job creation from ADB operations in Fiji, Indonesia, and Thailand using alternative approaches. Section 4 is an introspective on gaps in data and model application for further attention, and introduces possible remedial measures to improve jobs impact assessments. Section 5 concludes this study.

Methodology 2

There is a wide range of methodologies used by international and bilateral development agencies to estimate the employment impacts of investment and development assistance. The United Kingdom development finance institution—CDC Group PLC—and the impact and sustainability consultant firm Steward Redqueen have developed a tool to estimate the total number of jobs created by private sector investments (MacGillivray and Lelijveld 2019). The tool requires five inputs: direct, full-time equivalent headcount and basic financial data (i.e., revenues, earnings, taxes, and wages). These inputs are fed into a set of multipliers derived from national social accounting matrices and labor force surveys (LFS) to yield an estimate of the total number of jobs in a given year. The total employment impacts that the model captures are (i) directly employed workers at the business level, i.e., in the company or project that sponsors have invested in (directly or through a fund); (ii) supply chain jobs in investee's direct and indirect suppliers; and (iii) induced jobs, created as a result of spending the wages earned by employees of the investee and its direct and indirect suppliers. For finance services and electricity investment projects, economy-wide jobs are generated through lending to businesses and individuals, supplying electricity to businesses, and increased productivity. This method draws its primary data from the financial statements of project sponsors and has limited applications in public sector projects and programmatic support.

The African Development Bank, Belgium Investment Company for Developing Countries, CDC Group PLC, Development Finance Institute Canada, the Netherlands Entrepreneurial Development Bank (FMO), and the private sector financing arm of Agence Française de Développement (Proparco) in collaboration with Steward Redqueen have further developed this model to measure and report on indirect job creation impact of development assistance. This open access model, called the "Joint Impact Model," has since been made publicly available for all impact investors and other interested parties. Based on an input–output (IO) model, it incorporates the financial flows of project(s) through an economy, and translates these into impacts on value added (salary, taxes, profits), employment (women and youth), and greenhouse emissions.

Kluve and Stöterau (2014) provide a good summary of methodologies used by the Deutsche Gesellschaft für Internationale Zusammenarbeit (GIZ) to convert the gross to net employment effects of all German development assistance programs. GIZ uses a bottom–up approach and incorporates counterfactual, substitution, and displacement effects in their estimations.[3]

---

[3]   Authors' consultations with GIZ revealed there are data completeness and verification issues and the methodology is still being fine-tuned.

IO models have some constraints, as highlighted by IFC (2013) and MacGillivray and Lelijveld (2019). Multipliers in IO models might overstate the initial impact of the intervention on the economy for the following reasons. First, in calculating the multipliers it is often assumed that trading patterns are fixed and that beneficiaries (firms, contractors, or households) will buy from and sell to local industries in the same proportion as firms do in the area, and that local suppliers can increase their output to supply the new firms. Second, incoming firms are not always a net new source of economic activity; in fact, they can take business away from existing firms. A shift in the source of energy production from fossil fuels to solar energy is a good example of the need for a "net effect" analysis.

In addition, the relationship between industries often varies and the indirect economic impacts conveyed by multipliers may not occur in the same way under any given circumstance. Models used to derive the IO tables are linear and do not allow (i) for increasing return to scale effects to be captured, (ii) for the possibility of substitution toward cheaper inputs, or (iii) for productivity increases. Moreover, there can be supply constraints and workers may not be readily available at a given time and place, which is particularly relevant in the case of skilled workers. Another limitation is that the multipliers represent a snapshot of an economy at a particular point in time. The pattern of employment growth can be affected by the age of companies in the sector, changes in their capital intensity, investment (capital accumulation) decisions, depreciation of capital, technology adoption, and productivity changes. Finally, the induced employment effects depend on (i) the fraction of income spent versus the fraction saved, and (ii) the fraction of income spent on locally produced goods versus imported goods and services (IFC 2013). The lower the wage income spent on locally produced goods, the lower the employment impact.

If the context of interventions (such as cross-border infrastructure, trade, investment, industrial policy, technology, and skills) lead to significant spillover effects on productivity, cost structures, prices, substitution effects, and behavioral responses from all economic agents (firms, industry, household, governments), then the application of a national computable general equilibrium (CGE) model or a global model such as the Global Trade Analysis Project (GTAP) may be more appropriate.[4]

The primary difference between an IO model and a CGE model is the partial economic analysis in IO modeling versus the general equilibrium analysis in CGE modeling. The IO model includes Leontief (1986) assumptions, hence it is silent about price (substitution) effects even within a partial equilibrium context. Both models are static and do not include adequate intertemporal resource allocation mechanisms including saving and investment decisions, a major drawback when performing dynamic analyses. With these caveats, a CGE model can be seen as more theoretically grounded and more CGE complete with micro-foundations than an IO or social accounting matrix model. The CGE model allows for framing and assessing additional processes (such as the investment-capital accumulation process) and channels, including macroeconomic effects. It also has some drawbacks. It requires more extensive data and higher levels of technical skills to develop the model, run the model, and interpret its results. Further, "general equilibrium" is a theoretical expediency, rather than a depiction of actual market conditions. It may be argued that a CGE model is less transparent compared to the simpler construct of an IO model, and its outputs are quite sensitive to assumptions and choice of model closures. These, in turn, may have additional cost implications (Steward Redqueen 2021). This study explores

---

[4]   More information can be found at the GTAP website: https://www.gtap.agecon.purdue.edu/.

whether using CGE models would improve estimation accuracy (compared to IO models), using operations data from ADB's Fiji, Indonesia, and Thailand operations.

In this study, while developing a methodology that can be readily applied to ADB operations, both IO and CGE models were applied to portfolio data from three pilot countries for 2010-2019, to estimate the impact of ADB interventions on indirect and induced employment. The GTAP and national CGE models were used to check whether the employment impact derived through the IO model differs significantly from the estimates of the GTAP-CGE model.

The Input–Output Model for Employment Impact Analyses

An IO table provides a complete picture of the flow of products (goods and services) in the economy for a given year. It details the relationship between producers and consumers, and the interdependencies of industries. The table is the main tool used in IO-based impact analyses.

The relationship between product outputs, intermediate inputs (technology coefficient matrix A), and the final demand is given by:

$$AX + Y = X \tag{1}$$

where X is the vector of output, A is the IO coefficient matrix, and Y is the vector of final demand. Solving (1) for X gives:

$$X = (I - A)^{-1} Y \tag{2}$$

If there is an increase in final demand, say ΔY, the total impacts on output is given by:

$$\Delta X = (I - A)^{-1} \Delta Y \tag{3}$$

where $(I - A)^{-1}$ is called the Leontief Inverse or multiplier matrix, which is assumed to be stable.

Direct, Indirect, and Induced Effects and Multipliers

In IO analysis, the direct impact is assumed to be initiated by an exogenous increase in net final demand like an increase in export demand or an increase in fixed capital formation. It could also be an increase in domestic production of intermediate consumption to replace imports, an increase in indirect taxes, a change in technology represented by changes in input structures, etc. For example, the effect of the production of a motor vehicle does not end with the steel, tires, and other components required. It generates a long chain of interaction in the production process, since each of the products used as inputs needs to be produced first and will—in turn—require various inputs. The production of tires, for instance, requires rubber, steel, etc., which in turn require various products as inputs including the transport services provided by motor vehicles that necessitated the production of tires in the first place. One cycle of input requirement triggers another cycle of inputs, which in turn requires another cycle of input requirements. This chain of interactions goes into infinity. The sum of all these chain reactions is determined from the value of the Leontief inverse (United Nations 1999).

If there is an increase in final demand for a particular industry product, it can be assumed that there will be an equivalent increase in the output of that industry as it reacts to meet the increased demand. This is the *direct effect*, $\Delta_0 X = \Delta Y$, where Δ_n stands for sequences of change in output in responses to the initial change in final demand.

The chain of reaction of the effects can be simplified as follows:

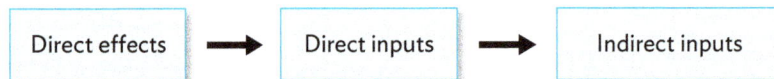

Direct effects → Direct inputs → Indirect inputs

Direct effects initially result in the requirement for direct inputs, which then trigger a chain of indirect inputs. The sum of direct inputs and indirect inputs is called "indirect effects."

The chain reactions generated by an increase in net final demand include a string of outputs. In the first round, it is the incremental output to meet the increase in net final demand. In the second round, it is the incremental output to meet the input requirement of production to meet the increase in net final demand. In the third round, it is the incremental output to meet the input requirement of the incremental output of the second round. The number of rounds goes on to infinity. Since the coefficient matrix A describes the input requirement of any increase in output, the chain reactions can be written as follows:

Exogenous shock: $\Delta_0 X = \Delta Y$ *direct effect*

The first-round effect: $\Delta_1 X = A \, \Delta Y$

The second round: $\Delta_2 X = A \times A \, \Delta Y = A^2 \Delta Y$

The third round: $\Delta_3 X = A^3 \Delta Y$

....   *indirect effect*

n^{th} round: $\Delta_n X = A^n \Delta Y$

The total impact (gross output generated) = *Direct effects + Indirect effects*

$$\Delta_0 X + \Delta_1 X + \Delta_2 X + ... + \Delta_n X = \Delta Y + A\Delta Y + A^2 \Delta Y + A^3 \Delta Y + ... + A^n \Delta Y$$
$$= (I + A + A^2 + A^3 + ... + A^n)\Delta Y$$
$$\text{or } \Delta X = (I - A)^{-1} \Delta Y$$

The output change per unit change of final demand: $\dfrac{\Delta X}{\Delta Y} = (I - A)^{-1}$ is called the output multiplier, the column sum of $(I - A)^{-1}$ is called "Type I multiplier," which includes both direct and indirect effects.

If households earn labor income from direct and indirect effects and spend them on the products produced by the industries, the industries and households are connected by this income-consumption relationship. This is done through modifying model (1) by adding a row of labor income and (endogenizing) household consumption to the column of matrix A, giving matrix B, and solving for output change in other final demands. The column sum of the solution matrix $(I - B)^{-1}$ is called "Type II multiplier."

As a result of these direct and indirect effects, the level of household income throughout the domestic economy will increase with increasing employment. A proportion of this increased income will be re-spent on domestically produced products, inducing another round of effect, i.e., the induced effect.[5] The induced effect is equal to the difference between the Type II multiplier and the Type I multiplier.

Output Multipliers

The output multiplier for an industry is expressed as the ratio of direct and indirect output changes to the direct output change due to a unit increase in final use. This means that multiplying a change in final use (direct impact) for an individual industry output by that industry's Type I output multiplier will generate an estimate of direct and indirect impacts upon output throughout the economy, and additional induced impacts if that industry Type II output multiplier is used (Scottish Goverment 2022).

Employment Effects and Multipliers

Employment effects show the direct plus indirect (plus induced, if Type II multipliers are used) employment changes to the direct output change, due to a unit increase in final use. If the industry output changes, the employment effect can be used to calculate the change in full-time equivalent (FTE) for the economy as a whole.[6]

$$\Delta L = \Delta X \times a_L = (I - A)^{-1} \Delta Y \times a_L \tag{4}$$

where a_L is the vector of employment per industry output.

The employment multiplier—expressed as FTE—is the ratio of direct plus indirect (plus induced, if Type II multipliers are used) employment changes to the direct employment change. If there is a direct change in FTE employment for the industry, the employment multiplier can be used to calculate the change in total FTE employment for the economy (footnote 5).

Input–Output Tables for Fiji, Indonesia, and Thailand

Key data sources for IO models used in this study are national IO tables. For this study, we have used ADB's multi-regional input–output tables (MRIOTs) from 2007 to 2019. The tables cover 63 countries and regions, and 35 industries, presented as a matrix of 35 rows and 35 columns. The data are presented in 2021 prices. MRIOT does not include a breakdown of gross value added (labor compensation or consumption of fixed capital).

---

[5] Y is matrix of final demand that include government, investment, and exports. Only household consumption is endogenized with labor income to derive induced effect (footnote 2).

[6] Full-time equivalent employment is the number of full-time equivalent jobs—defined as total hours actually worked by all employed persons—divided by the average number of hours actually worked in a full-time job. Further information is available at Scottish Government. 2022. Supply, Use and Input-Output Tables. 26 October. https://www.gov.scot/publications/about-supply-use-input-output-tables/pages/user-guide-introduction/.

The Eora Gobal Supply Chain Database consists of a multi-regional input–output (MRIO) model that provides a time series of high-resolution IO tables with matching environmental and social satellite accounts for 190 countries. The Eora MRIO features a balanced global MRIOT documenting the inter-sector transfers amongst 15,909 sectors across 190 countries, a complete time series for 1990–2015, and 2720-line-item environmental indicators. It also includes labor compensation.

The World Input–Output Database provides world IO tables in 2021 prices, denoted in millions of dollars. The database covers 28 European Union countries and 15 other major countries in the world from 2000 to 2014. The structure of the data is similar to ADB MRIOs.

The latest GTAP 10 database comprises data on 141 countries and regions for 65 sectors and describes the world economy for 4 reference years (2004, 2007, 2011, and 2014). The countries in the database account for 98% of the world gross domestic product (GDP) and 92% of the world population. For each country or region, the database reports production, intermediate and final uses, international trade and transport margins, and taxes and/or subsidies (Aguiar et al. 2019). The data also include labor compensation for five occupations: officials and managers, technicians and associated professionals, clerks, service and shop workers, agricultural and unskilled workers.

To apply the IO model for employment impact analyses, a series of IO tables and detailed employment data from the labor force surveys are required. More detailed and disaggregated IO tables improve the robustness of analyses. Sources and availability of data are summarized in Table 1.

Table 1: Required Data for Employment Impact Analyses with Input–Output Model

		Input–Output Tables		Labor Force Surveys	
	Year	Number of Sectors	Source	Frequency	Source
Indonesia	2010	185	Statistics Indonesia (BPS)	Monthly	Statistics Indonesia (BPS)
	2004, 2007, 2011, and 2014	65	GTAP		
	2007–2019	35	ADB		
	1990–2015	26	Eora		
Fiji	2007–2019	35	ADB	Annual (Paid) Employment Survey The Employment and Unemployment Survey (EUS)—every 5 years	Fiji Bureau of Statistics
	2011 and 2015	116	USP		
	1990–2015	26	Eora		
Thailand	2005	180	NESDB	4 times per year since 1998	National Statistical Office
	2004, 2007, 2011, and 2014	65	GTAP		
	2007–2019	35	ADB		
	2000–2014	56	WIOT		
	1990–2015	26	Eora		

ADB = Asian Development Bank, BPS = Badan Pusat Statistik, EUS = Employment and Unemployment Survey, GTAP = Global Trade Analysis Project, NESDB = National Economic and Social Development Board, USP = University of the South Pacific, WIOT = World Input–Output Tables.
Source: Authors' compilations.

The large inter-regional CGE model of Indonesia—based on the Australian "the enormous regional model" (TERM)—distinguishing all 30 provinces and up to 179 sectors, was used to analyze improving domestic connectivity.

The latest 185-sector national IO table in 2010 for Indonesia was published by Statistics Indonesia (BPS). In addition, the IndoLab can construct time-series MRIOTs from 1990 to 2015, capturing up to 1148 sectors and 495 regions and consisting of five value-added and six final-demand categories.

Thailand has produced benchmark national IO tables since 1975, and it has been compiled regularly every 5 years. Its first IO table was compiled by the office of the National Economic and Social Development Board in cooperation with Chulalongkorn University, the National Statistical Office, and the Institute of Developing Economies, Japan (Kwangmoon et al. 2011). The latest 180-sector national IO table is for 2005.

The Fiji Bureau of Statistics uses an updated IO table. Starting with the Fiji 2011 supply-use table, a representative IO of the Fiji economy was updated to 106 sector IO tables in 2011 and 2015 by Oum and Singh (2019). These tables were used to inform the CGE model.

The starting point of the employment assessment is the 35-sector IO table estimated by ADB from 2010 to 2019 (Appendix 1, Table A1.1). The tables were supplemented by labor force surveys to be able to estimate the job creation impact by industry and gender.

Employment Impact Analyses

To use the IO model for the selected countries, how projects and programmatic interventions in these countries would directly affect final demand for domestically produced goods and services or industry output, productivity, firm revenues, household income, and employment (direct impact) need to be identified. By mapping these direct impacts per industry and using the corresponding multipliers of the IO models, the total impact on employment can be estimated and distinguished by direct, indirect, and induced employment impact. The employment impact analyses are made by comparing ADB operations' employment effects with a counterfactual situation where the said ADB operations do not exist. In other words, the impacts being assessed are employment outcomes that could not have materialized without the said ADB operations in a given ADB member.

Using detailed information on sector employment from labor force surveys, the model can then be used to estimate employment impact by type of occupation, gender, full-time and part-time jobs, and formal and informal jobs (figure on Employment Impact Analysis).[7]

As noted by MacGillivray and Lelijveld (2019), job quality is not easy to measure. Therefore, decent work would need to be proxied by a link between formal or informal categories and decent work, albeit with nuanced differences in definition. Employment is generally defined in terms of any work

---

[7] If IO tables include the informal sector and the proportion of jobs that are formal and informal by sector are included in national labor force surveys, this would allow for separate estimates of formal and informal employment impacts by sector.

Employment Impact Analysis

```
                    Projects and Policy
                       Interventions
                            │
                            ▼
                       Direct Impacts
   (Final Demand, Output, Revenue, Income, Employment, Productivity, etc.)
                            │
                            ▼
                       Input-Output
                          Model
                            │
        ┌───────────────────┼───────────────────┐
        ▼                    ▼                    ▼
  Direct Employment   Indirect Employment   Induced Employment
```

Source: Authors.

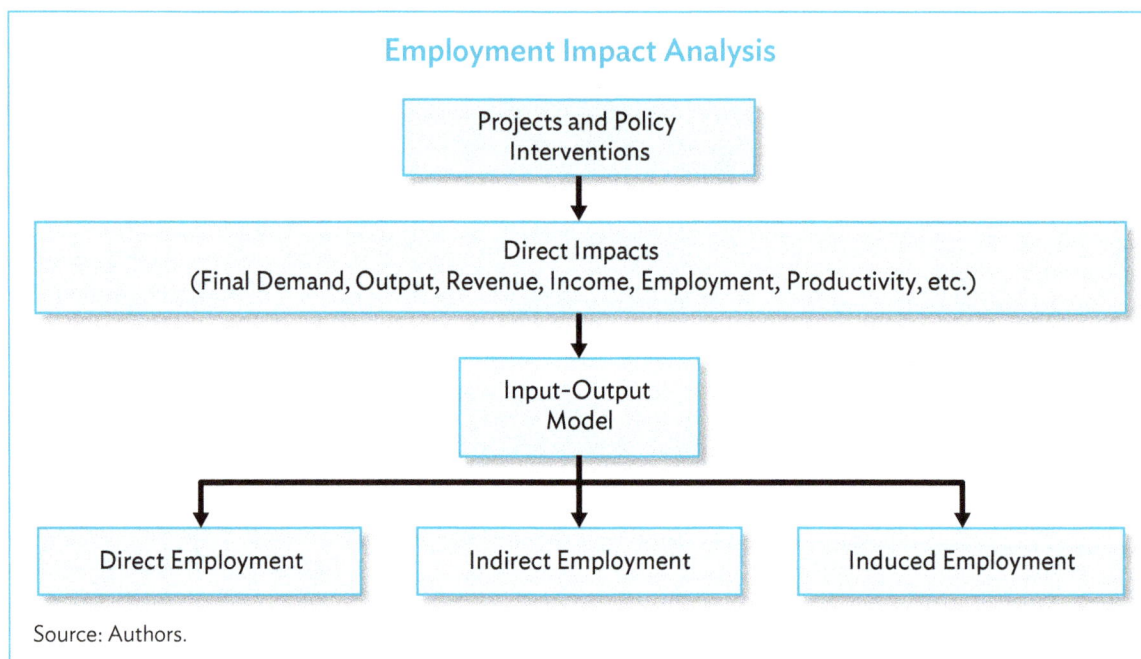

during the relevant period (e.g., 2 hours of work during the 2 weeks preceding the survey interview), not full-time work (Bourmpoula, Gomis, and Kapsos 2017). This means that a projection of the number of jobs created from a given intervention indicates any sort of employment or income-generating activity, and not necessarily full-time jobs. Hence, it is preferable to indicate FTE jobs in the model or use a conversion factor (ILO 2020).[8]

Caution should also be taken about "net" job creation, as new firms can create new jobs, but they can also cause job losses for their competitors, and this can affect overall job creation and employment level in an industry. In countries with very high unemployment rates, job creation will usually be in the form of drawing new entrants—previously under-employed or unemployed people—into the labor force. In countries with large informal sectors, creating formal sector jobs may pull workers from the informal into the formal sector. And in countries that are already close to full employment, job creation will likely come in the form of attracting workers into higher value-added jobs that offer higher wages and benefits (IFC 2013).

This report could only provide the "estimates of potential job creation" in the formal sector (as a proxy for decent jobs created). It is a "gross," not "net job creation" effect from ADB operations in the three selected countries. Having said that, given the nature of ADB interventions to address infrastructure deficit and policy gaps in its members, the likelihood of job or business destruction would be minimal.

---

[8]   Appendix 5 shows employment multipliers.

Estimation of Direct Impacts

The direct impacts of investment projects or policy interventions need to be identified in the three selected countries. Once the direct impacts are identified, the corresponding multipliers of the IO models can be used to estimate the economy-wide impact on employment.

Direct impacts can differ by type of interventions, sector beneficiaries, type of infrastructure, and business environments. At the project level, an estimation of direct employment for a project requires the project's expenditure information, technology and scale, as well as the typical employment per dollar spent for the particular type of project.

For example, the data on employment and expenditure of the projects can be directly collected. Or they can be tabulated and estimated by industry or research institutions from historical survey data on typical characteristics of a given industry, project design specifications, and data for representative plants. Key factors in ascertaining the direct employment impacts of a project are the degree to which manufacturing will be carried out domestically and the duration of the project. A further distinction is made between employment for construction, installation, and manufacturing, and employment for operation and maintenance (Bacon and Kojima 2011).

For the private sector, expansion of business activities often requires investments in new construction, equipment, or software. Because these purchases constitute changes in final demand rather than changes in intermediate inputs, the impacts of these purchases need to be estimated separately. Investment impacts can be added to the impacts resulting from expanded operations associated with a project. The purchase of a new machine should not be included in the final-demand change that is applied to the multipliers for new construction. This is because the said machine is not an intermediate purchase for the construction industry. Instead, the value of the new machine should be multiplied by the final-demand multipliers for the industry that manufactures the machines (Bess and Ambargis 2011).

Based on the information from the ADB operations database and relevant information on sector classification (Table 2), it is feasible to conduct the ex ante and ex post analyses of the potential impacts of these projects and programs on job creation in the selected countries.

It is crucial to have an accurate estimate of direct jobs resulting from investment and other types of development assistance projects. The total of estimated direct jobs may be attained from two sources: (i) the reported direct job creation during the construction and operation period, or (ii) the model's estimate based on direct domestic purchase of non-construction capital goods under the project. In the latter case, detailed information on construction and capital expenditure for specific projects (domestic and imported) are required to estimate the direct, indirect, and induced effects.

Table 2: ADB Program and Project Classification

	Sector	Theme	Status/Year
1	Agriculture, natural resources, and rural development	Environmentally sustainable growth	Proposed Retrofitted Approved Active Dropped/Terminated Closed
2	Education	Gender Equity and Mainstreaming	
3	Energy	Governance and capacity development	
4	Finance	Inclusive economic growth	
5	Health	Knowledge solutions	
6	Health and social protection	Partnerships	
7	Industry and trade	Private sector development	
8	Information and communication technology	Regional integration	
9	Multisector		
10	Public sector management		
11	Transport		
12	Transport and ICT		
13	Water and other urban infrastructure and services		

ADB = Asian Development Bank, ICT = information and communications technology.
Source: ADB.

Estimation of Direct Jobs Using the Model

Data availability and consistency have been flagged as a gap early on in these analyses. When direct job creation data are not available from project or program documents, the direct job creation during the construction and operation of such projects can be estimated from the average employment per output for sample projects in a specific country. For example, workers per installation of 1 megawatt in solar, wind, or coal-based power plants, or number of workers per 1 kilometer of road. Another approach is to use the allocated amount for construction, non-capital expenditure, and the output-to-employment ratio of the model to derive an estimate for direct jobs created.

For those projects without detailed domestic procurement information, these amounts are assumed to follow the patterns of the model for non-construction capital expenditures.

Not all ADB sovereign projects monitor and report on direct job creation during project implementation. The project administration manual provides for some cost estimates by expenditure category, mainly on civil works, equipment, and management services. These project expenditures are treated as capital formation expenditure, as in the IO model, to derive the direct, indirect, and induced employment effects.

In this case, direct jobs estimate for industry i is given by the formula:

$$Direct\ Job_i = Final\ Demand\ for\ Industy\ Output, \Delta Y_i \times Jobs\ per\ Industry\ Output, a_{Li} \qquad (5)$$

or

$$Direct\ Job_i = (Project\ Cost_i \times Share\ of\ Capital\ Expenditure) \times Jobs\ per\ Industry\ Output, a_{Li}$$

using equation (4) or employment multiplier to estimate the total job impacts:

$$\Delta L = [(I - A)^{(-1)} \Delta Y] \times a_{(L_i)}$$

or

$$\Delta L = Direct\ Jobs_i \times Employment\ Multiplier_i$$

where $Direct\ Jobs_i$ is the estimated direct job creation from the project industry i, *Share of Capital Expenditure* is capital expenditure share of the industry in the IO model, and a is the coefficient of industrial employment per output.

It is important to note that using the model employment per output to derive the number of direct jobs created can compromise the actual direct impacts due to the significant differences between project level employment per investment cost and the employment per industry output estimated by the model, as shown on pages 29–36.

ADB Attribution and Annualized Estimates

Since many of the projects are cofinanced, direct jobs created and total job creation are adjusted according to the share of ADB financing in the total project cost to derive the ADB share of job creation. These are then annualized with the following formula:

$$Annualized\ Direct\ Jobs_i = (Direct\ Jobs_i \times Share_{ADB}) / Years \qquad (6)$$

where $Share_{ADB}$ is the share of ADB contribution in the total project finance, and *Years* is the duration of the project construction.[9]

The annualized capital expenditure of an ADB-financed project is given by:

$$Annualized\ Project\ Capital\ Expenditure_i = \qquad (7)$$
$$(Project\ Cost_i \times Share_{ADB} \times Share\ of\ Capital\ Expenditure\ in\ project\ cost) / Years$$

---

[9]   Land purchase is excluded in this case—and any associated capital expenditure by the project for land purchase—as the focus is on investments that generate additional jobs.

Total Jobs by Gender

Total employment disaggregated by gender is estimated with project data on direct jobs created, IO model estimates of indirect and induced jobs, and the fixed employment ratio of female to total employed in that industry:

$$Total\,Job_{(female)_i} = [Direct\,Job_i + Indirect\,Job_i + Induced\,Job_i] \times Share_{(female/total)_i} \qquad (8)$$

where $Share_{(female/total)_i}$ is the fixed employment ratio of females employed in the industry to the total number of males and females employed.

Alternative Approaches to Measure Jobs Impact

3

This section discusses estimation of jobs that would potentially have been created as a result of ADB operations in Fiji, Indonesia, and Thailand by using alternative approaches, compares results attained and explores whether some of these approaches may be applicable to budget support programs. Appendixes 3 to 5 shows the value of wages, number of jobs, and the amount of ADB operations in these countries. The data used in this section are also drawn from Fiji Bureau of Statistics (2018) for Fiji, Faturay et al. (2017) for Indonesia, and Kwangmoon et al. (2011) and Papong (2015) for Thailand.

Fiji

Employment and wages. Matching employment and wage data of Fiji to ADB 35 by 35 industry MRIOTs during 2010–2019 is a challenge because of incomplete data from the Fiji Employment and Unemployment Surveys published by the Fiji Bureau of Statistics in 2017 and 2018. Published survey reports provide employment data for 2010, 2011, 2014, 2015, 2016, 2017, and 2018. To fill the data gap for 2012 and 2013, employment rates were derived from the World Bank's *World Development Indicators* and applied to estimate sector employment for 2012 and 2013.[10] Employment data only include wage and salary employment. Informal employment—which is estimated to account for more than 40% of total employment in Fiji—is not reported. This study includes only formal sector employment data.

The *Fiji Gross Domestic Product 2017 Income Approach Report* was used for wage data, which provided the share of compensation of employees by industries during 2010–2019 (Fiji Bureau of Statistics 2018). The wage and employment data are only available for 21 industries that are mapped with the 35 industries included in MRIOTs.[11]

Summary of ADB operations. During 2010–2019, ADB had approved and implemented nine sovereign technical assistance (TA) projects, two grants, and nine program loans; there were no nonsovereign operations (Table 3). The nine TA projects provided $6.36 million for three public sector projects, two transport and water sector projects, one energy sector, and one information and communication technology project. A total of $2 million in grants supported public sector management.

---

[10] World Bank. World Development Indicators. https://datatopics.worldbank.org/world-development-indicators/ (accessed 20 October 2021).

[11] Appendixes 4 and 5 have more information on data referenced in this section.

Table 3: ADB Projects in Fiji, 2010–2019

	Sector	Technical Assistance		Grant		Sovereign Loan	Finance ($ million)	
		No.	$ million	No.	$ million	No.	ADB	Non-ADB
1	Energy	1	1.20					
2	Transport	2	1.00			2	127.5	61.8
3	Public Sector	3	1.98	2	2	3	130.0	130.0
4	Water	2	1.96			3	178.7	235.8
5	Other	1	0.23			1	17.6	2.4
	Total	**9**	**6.36**	**2**	**2**	**9**	**453.7**	**430.0**

ADB = Asian Development Bank, No. = number.

Note: Numbers may not sum precisely because of rounding.

Sources: ADB. Sovereign Projects. https://data.adb.org/dataset/adb-sovereign-projects (accessed 20 October 2021); and ADB. Projects & Tenders. https://www.adb.org/projects (accessed 20 October 2021).

Among the nine sovereign loans, three were policy-based loans, two of which were for sustained private sector-led growth reform programs and the third one was on emergency assistance for recovery from Tropical Cyclone Winston. Three projects were on water supply investment and management, two projects on the transport sector for road upgrading and transport infrastructure investment, and one project on emergency flood recovery. Further project details are provided in Appendix 2.

Job creation from ADB operations. ADB operations in Fiji included capital investments and program lending to the public sector during 2010–2019. For this study, all non-program loans are treated as capital investments—mostly in infrastructure—and the pattern of gross capital formulation in the IO model is used as the basis of job impact estimation in the absence of jobs impact data from project and program documents.

The ADB portfolio in Fiji included seven sovereign projects in 2010, 2014, 2015, and 2016. The total cost of these seven projects was $746.7 million, of which ADB funded $373 million (Table 4).

Table 4: Investment Projects in Fiji, 2010–2019
($ million)

Year	Total	ADB
2010	115.6	67.4
2014	116.7	100.0
2015	9.4	2.7
2016	505.1	203.0
Total	**746.7**	**373.0**

ADB = Asian Development Bank.

Note: Numbers may not sum precisely because of rounding.

Sources: ADB. Projects & Tenders. https://www.adb.org/projects (accessed 20 October 2021); and authors' estimates.

Estimated direct jobs for all projects during 2010–2019 are provided by sector in Appendix 1, Table A1.6. The estimates for economy-wide total job creation for Fiji are reported in Appendix 1, Table A1.7. Direct jobs created are estimated at 11,669 (3,479 female) and 5,673 jobs (1,682 female) were attributable to ADB funding. When data were annualized, it was estimated that 200 (51 female) direct jobs were created per year.

It is estimated that 15,785 jobs were created through these investments during 2010–2019. Female employment accounted for 4,669 FTEs of job creation. Total jobs created included an estimated 11,669 direct jobs. Indirect jobs were estimated to be 3,513 (1,031 female) and induced jobs were estimated to be 603 (177 female). ADB contributions led to 7,622 jobs (2,265 female) or an average of 278 jobs per year (73 female) during this decade.

Table 5 shows the distribution of total job creation between construction and non-construction related expenditures per year. Direct jobs comprised about 72.6% of the total (25.6% female), indirect jobs accounted for 23.6% (28.1% female) and induced effects accounted for 4.4% (29.7% female) of the total jobs created. Jobs created for women accounted for 26.3% of the total job creation on an annual basis.

Table 5: Estimate of Annualized Total Job Creation by Sector from ADB Projects in Fiji, 2010–2019
(full-time equivalent)

Sector	Direct		Indirect		Induced		Total	
	All	Female	All	Female	All	Female	All	Female
Construction	193	8	14	1	1	0	209	9
Others	202	65	83	24	16	5	300	94
Average	**200**	**51**	**66**	**18**	**12**	**4**	**278**	**73**
	72.6% of Total	25.6% of all direct	23.6% of Total	28.1% of all indirect	4.4% of Total	29.7% of all induced	100%	26.3% of Total

ADB = Asian Development Bank.
Note: Numbers may not sum precisely because of rounding.
Sources: ADB. Projects & Tenders. https://www.adb.org/projects (accessed 20 October 2021); and authors' estimates.

The share of direct jobs is higher in Fiji compared to Thailand and Indonesia, as it will be further demonstrated in the succeeding sections. This is due to the underlying assumption that all investments in transport, water, and reconstruction from cyclone destruction would go to construction and other purchases of capital goods. Since the import content of capital expenditure is high for Fiji, the indirect and induced impacts on the domestic economy are relatively lower than the impacts observed in Indonesia and Thailand.

Indonesia

Employment and wages. ADB's MRIOTs do not include labor compensation and employment for Indonesia. In this study, employment and wage data from 17 sectors of the *Laborer Situation Indonesia* published by BPS Statistics Indonesia were used to derive and match with the 35 sector MRIOTs for Indonesia during 2010–2019.

Summary of ADB operations. During 2010–2019, ADB approved and implemented 69 sovereign TA projects, 2 grants, 37 sovereign loans, and 9 nonsovereign loans (Table 6). The 69 TA projects provided $16.7 million of support, with energy (15), agriculture (16), public sector (13), and finance sector (9) as the top recipients; and public sector management was supported with grants totaling $3 million.

Table 6: ADB Projects in Indonesia, 2010–2019

	Sector	Technical Assistance		Grant		Sovereign Loan	Finance ($ million)		Nonsovereign Loan	Finance ($ million)	
		No.	$ million	No.	$ million	No.	ADB	Non-ADB	No.	ADB	Non-ADB
1	Energy	15	1.1			8	2,498.5	2,416.0	7	1,333.9	3,189.7
2	Finance	9	1.9			5	1,700.8	0.0	1	100.0	100.0
3	Transport	5	1.5			3	881.0	700.5	0		
4	Public Sector	13	6.3	2	3.0	9	3,347.8	1,374.7	0		
5	Agriculture	16	2.2			7	1,300.2	1,198.7	0		
6	Education	5	2.0			2	275.0	83.2	0		
7	Others[a]	6	1.7			3	189.4	286.2	1	10.0	10.0
	Total	**69**	**16.7**	**2**	**3.0**	**37**	**10,192.6**	**6,059.3**	**9**	**1,443.9**	**3,299.7**

ADB = Asian Development Bank, No. = number.
Note: Numbers may not sum precisely because of rounding.
[a] Includes health sector
Sources: ADB. Sovereign Projects. https://data.adb.org/dataset/adb-sovereign-projects (accessed 20 October 2021); and ADB. Projects & Tenders. https://www.adb.org/projects (accessed 20 October 2021).

In sharp contrast to its predominantly nonsovereign operations in Thailand, the majority of ADB support to Indonesia was allocated through 37 sovereign loans worth more than $16 billion. Sovereign loans were provided for programmatic support, energy, finance, and agriculture sector projects. Energy was also prominent in nonsovereign operations, with seven of the nine nonsovereign loans directed to the energy sector, and two projects focused on finance and health sectors. Detailed portfolio information are provided in Appendix 3.

Job creation from ADB operations. Direct, indirect, and induced job creation have been estimated for ADB sovereign and nonsovereign projects and programs in Indonesia. TA projects (mostly advisory and capacity development technical assistance) were not included while estimating jobs created in this study.

All ADB nonsovereign projects support estimates of direct job creation during the construction and operation periods—as reported in project design and review reports—and take into account domestic purchases made for the project during the construction period.

Policy-based and other programmatic lending, on the other hand, provide budgetary support for policy reforms and cross-sector development agendas. Their impact on jobs is not readily available, unless specified and tagged in advance during program design and quantified in ex post results assessments. Some of the outcomes are linked with Indonesian sector or macroeconomic indicators, where attribution would require comprehensive information about all financing partners for the targeted sectors or countrywide systems, which are not always recorded or reported in program documents. Hence, a two-phased approach was taken with program loans. Some program loans have been disbursed and closed with limited opportunities to generate program-specific employment-linked information. The estimation model discussed previously will be applied to the investment in Indonesia.

A summary of total investments by type of project, an estimate of domestic purchases made under the projects, and a share of ADB contributions to project cost are provided in Table 7.

The reported and estimated direct jobs for all ADB investment projects during 2010–2019 by sector are in Appendix 1. Total direct jobs created during 2010–2019 are estimated to be 356,029 for the investment portfolio summarized in Table 7, with 79,218 FTEs of direct female employment.

Table 7: Investment Projects in Indonesia, 2010–2019

| | Sovereign Project | | | Nonsovereign Project | | | | |
| | Investment ($ million) | | | Investment ($ million) | | Estimated Local Purchase ($ million) | | |
Year	Total	ADB	ADB Annualized	Total	ADB	Total	ADB	ADB Annualized
2010	164.5	85.0	20.2	–	–	–	–	–
2011	480.5	280.0	45.7	200.0	100.0	–	–	–
2012	152.2	132.5	20.8			–	–	–
2013	522.2	319.0	51.3	1,239.0	330.0	200.0	53.3	13.3
2014	412.1	154.4	21.3	50.0	50.0	10.0	6.0	10.0
2015	600.0	575.0	143.8					
2016	329.2	256.9	52.6	990.9	470.0	270.0	189.5	94.8
2017	3,381.0	1,100.0	203.3	120.8	56.4	41.0	19.1	9.6
2018	266.5	200.0	40.0	2,302.8	437.5	232.0	55.7	26.9
2019	455.2	378.0	90.0			–	–	
Total	**6,763.3**	**3,480.8**	**688.9**	**4,903.5**	**1,443.9**	**753.0**	**323.6**	**154.5**

ADB = Asian Development Bank.
Note: Numbers may not be exact due to rounding.
Sources: ADB. Projects & Tenders. https://www.adb.org/projects (accessed 20 October 2021); and authors' estimates.

Using the IO model, an estimated 108,611 FTEs for total direct jobs were generated through nonsovereign projects, compared to the 25,466 targeted at the project design stage and as noted in project documents. The difference is due to the inclusion of direct jobs from the purchase of non-construction goods (other non-intermediate, capital goods) in the model, but not in the project design and monitoring documents. ADB support accounted for 173,134 of the total direct jobs (35,904 female) or an average of 4,710 jobs per year (1,092 female), as estimated using the IO model.

A total of 724,917 jobs were created from all projects during 2010–2019. Indirect jobs created were estimated to be 316,329 (102,206 female). For the same period, it is estimated that 52,558 FTEs (19,250 female) of induced jobs were created. Furthermore, nonsovereign projects accounted for 178,046 FTEs of all jobs created, of which 200,674 were female FTEs. Detailed estimates for total job creation in Indonesia are provided in Appendix 1, Table A1.5.

The contribution of ADB to total jobs created is estimated to be 363,890 (97,730 female) or an average of 9,438 jobs per year (2,486 female), after adjusting for the construction period of the projects.

Table 8 provides the sector distribution of annualized job creation by direct, indirect, and induced effects for the rest of the economy. Estimated direct job creation is about 50% of the total (23.2% female), whereas the induced effects account for 43% of total job creation (29% female) as compared to 7% of the indirect job creation (33.5% female). Female workers account for about 26.3% of jobs created on average per year.

Table 8: Estimate of Annualized Total Job Creation by Sector from ADB-Funded Projects in Indonesia, 2010–2019

Sector	Direct			Indirect			Induced			Total		
	All	NS	Female	All	NS	Female	All	NS	Female	All	NS	Female
Construction	1,818	846	42	830	1,577	19	103	202	2	2,751	2,625	64
Energy	36	36	6	54	78	9	10	14	2	100	129	17
Transport	54	69	4	175	51	12	28	15	2	257	135	17
Others	2,823	3,536	1,044	3,004	875	1,132	523	287	217	6,350	4,698	2,392
Total	**4,710**	**4,487**	**1,092**	**4,064**	**2,581**	**1,172**	**664**	**518**	**222**	**9,438**	**7,587**	**2,486**
	49.9% of Total	95.3% of all direct	23.2% of all direct	43.1% of Total	63.5% of all indirect	28.8% of all indirect	7.0% of Total	78.1% of all induced	33.5% of all induced	100%	80.4% of Total	26.3% of Total

ADB = Asian Development Bank, NS = nonsovereign operations.
Note: Numbers may not sum precisely because of rounding.
Sources: ADB. Projects & Tenders. https://www.adb.org/projects (accessed 20 October 2021); and authors' estimates.

ADB operations seem to have had greater direct and indirect impacts on jobs in Indonesia compared to the same period of operations in Thailand. But the share of induced jobs is relatively lower. This is possibly due to input data used for the model. The lower share of estimated direct jobs in Thailand is due to the separation of reported direct jobs from the project cost and the assumption of the pattern of domestic purchase. The direct jobs are mainly generated from the construction and operation of the mostly energy projects, while the domestic purchase would generate a greater number of indirect and induced jobs. In the case of Indonesia, the source of direct jobs came from both the construction of the nonsovereign investment and the final demand for capital goods for the assumed sovereign investment projects. The amount of capital goods demand appeared to be much greater. Another reason was the extent of the inter-industrial linkages and the different sector multipliers in the two countries. It was observed that the higher the multipliers were, the larger the indirect and induced impacts became.

Thailand

Employment and wages. To estimate the impact of ADB projects on employment, the IO model was used for Thailand with ADB MRIOTs, labor compensation, and employment data from Thailand labor force surveys (LFS).[12]

First, a concordance—or mapping—between the industrial classification in the ADB MRIOTs and Thailand LFS was created. In the mapping process, it was noted that some industries of one dataset might be more disaggregated than the others. In such cases, the industrial shares of the disaggregated industries (gross value added or output) were used to split the aggregated ones.

The next step was to map wage and employment data from the 21 Thai industries' LFSs to the 35 industries included in the ADB MRIOTs. For example, to map the employment and wages of a given manufacturing industry from the LFS into the 15 concordant industries in the IO table, the share of output of each of these 15 industries was used to allocate their employment and wage from the said manufacturing industry LFS. The International Labour Organization (ILO) database was also used to estimate employment by gender in each industry.

The tables used to build the IO models and estimate employment impacts for Thailand during 2010–2019 only had 34 industries as there was no entry for "private households with employed persons."[13] With these matching labor compensation and employment with MRIOTs for Thailand, Multiplier Type I was used to estimate the direct and indirect impacts of project or policy interventions on employment, and Type II Multiplier as used to estimate induced employment, i.e., jobs created from the increased demand associated with extra income from labor compensation.

Summary of ADB operations. During 2010–2019, ADB approved and implemented 15 sovereign TA projects, 2 grants, 2 sovereign loans, and 21 nonsovereign loans in Thailand (Table 3). Of the 15 TA projects—totaling $5.1 million—six were for the finance sector, five for transport, and four for public sector management, water, and other urban infrastructure and services.

One sovereign loan of $300 million was extended to help develop the Thai capital market and support long-term, sustainable growth, focusing on the regulatory environment, market efficiency, liquidity and transparency, market infrastructure, and new products and investors. The second loan—the Greater Mekong Subregion Highway Expansion Project, approved for $99.4 million (together with $112 million

---

[12] Published data on employment and wages by the National Statistical Office of Thailand cover only 21 industries.

[13] Appendixes 2 and 5 have more information on data referenced in this section.

of the government budget)—helped upgrade about 142.5 kilometers of a two-lane national highway to a four-lane divided highway standard.

A total of 21 nonsovereign loans provided $1.75 billion in investment support (Table 9). Out of these projects, 16 were in the energy sector and supported the government's goal of increased energy supply (two 1,600-megawatt and two 2,500-megawatt gas-fired combined cycle power plants) and renewable energy targets (six solar, four wind power, and one biomass projects) with $1.34 billion.

Table 9: ADB Projects in Thailand, 2010–2019

		Technical Assistance		Grant		Sovereign Loan Finance ($ million)			Nonsovereign Loan Finance ($ million)		
	Sector	No.	$ million	No.	$ million	No.	ADB	Non-ADB	No.	ADB	Non-ADB
1	Energy								16	1,340.9	5,002.2
2	Finance	6	2.0			1	300.9		4	95.0	
3	Transport	5	2.0			1	99.4	112	1	318.0	2,642
4	Others	4	1.2	2	3.0						
	Total	**15**	**5.1**	**2**	**3.0**	**2**	**400.3**	**112**	**21**	**1,753.9**	**7,644.2**

ADB = Asian Development Bank, No. = number.

Note: Numbers may not sum precisely because of rounding.

Sources: ADB. Sovereign Projects. https://data.adb.org/dataset/adb-sovereign-projects (accessed 21 October 2021); and https://www.adb.org/projects (accessed 20 October 2021).

Four nonsovereign projects were approved with $95 million of ADB financing; three of which were for equity investments, and one supported a regional credit guarantee and investment facility. The last project provided $318 million financing for the construction and operation of the mass rapid transit (MRT) Pink Line and Yellow Line in Bangkok.

Job creation from ADB operations. TA projects and grants—mostly for advisory and capacity development assistance—can potentially support job creation if, for example, the policy reforms they support remove constraints to job creation and economic growth. To capture the potential job creation impact of TA projects, it would be important to include detailed outputs and outcomes related to job creation, preferably with quantifiable, time-bound targets. This is not the case for most TA projects in 2021, but ADB is reviewing TA templates and results frameworks to strengthen results capture for job creation support through ADB TA projects.

For this study, the direct, indirect, and induced job creation was estimated for sovereign and nonsovereign ADB projects and programs in Thailand.[14]

---

[14] Direct job creation could not be estimated for nine projects in the Thailand portfolio due to a lack of publicly available project data (confidentiality, pretermination, scope change, or cancellation of a project). Therefore, only 19 projects from the 2010–2019 portfolio have been used for job estimates (Appendix 4).

All 19 projects in the portfolio were in the energy and transport sectors, and their impact have been primarily through direct job creation during project construction and operation periods. Construction, operation, and maintenance of infrastructure assets create employment through three channels:

(i)   for workers to construct, operate, and maintain the assets (direct effect);
(ii)   for workers in related supply and distribution networks for the infrastructure asset being created (indirect effect); and
(iii) for workers who provide household consumption goods and services to (i) and (ii) (induced effect).

Construction impacts tend to be short term (limited to the construction period) and temporary. Operation and maintenance impacts start after construction is completed; they are both continuous and cumulative.

When an ADB intervention removes or modulates an existing binding constraint to growth, and the outcomes are captured, it is possible to estimate the resultant increase in jobs (or the second-order effects) that are created in different spheres of the economy. For instance, if an insufficient power supply is a binding constraint to growth, increasing power supply by investing in power generation and distribution could help generate more industrial production, economic growth, and hence employment (IFC 2013). As of 2021, ADB operational databases do not track this effect systematically.

In this analysis, job creation is estimated starting from the project approval year. It is important to note in this case: (i) that the construction period may include dormant periods for job creation, e.g., when construction does not start immediately or turnover for operations is delayed; and (ii) that labor elasticities within a sector or even during the construction cycle of a project may differ, e.g., construction of wind and solar power projects require shorter construction periods than large gas-fired, combined cycle power plants. Adjustments to key estimates were made. Typical construction and installation periods of solar and wind energy projects are about 3 to 8 months—depending on the size of the project—therefore the annualized equivalent is adjusted by converting month to job-year full-time direct jobs.

Three sets of estimations for direct, indirect, and induced job creation from total investments are presented here. The first set is the total job creation by the total amount of investment (with ADB and other financings) in a given year. The second set highlights only ADB contributions to total job creation, and the final set is the annualized contribution of ADB to total job creation.

Table 10 provides a summary of the total investments in Thailand during 2010-2019. During this decade, ADB financed $1.6 billion of the $9.4 billion total investments. The estimated local purchases were $3.14 billion, of which $743 million—$348 million per year—were financed by ADB.

The estimates of direct jobs incorporate jobs data from construction and operation periods as reported in project documents, project completion reports, extended annual review reports, and model estimates from direct domestic purchases.

Table 10: Investment Projects in Thailand, 2010–2019

Year	Investment ($ million)		Estimated Local Purchase ($ million)		
	Total	**ADB**	**Total**	**ADB**	**ADB-Annualized**
2010	215.0	215.0	105.0	105.0	105.0
2011	1,462.0	155.0	681.9	72.0	24.0
2012	1,563.3	181.0	788.2	81.1	29.7
2013	88.7	53.7	38.4	23.3	23.3
2014	83.0	53.0	36.9	23.5	11.8
2017	244.1	132.1	108.4	58.6	15.8
2018	4,265.6	700.6	726.3	314.0	90.7
2019	1,489.4	155.0	658.1	66.0	48.1
Total	**9,411.1**	**1,645.3**	**3,143.3**	**743.4**	**348.4**

ADB = Asian Development Bank.
Note: Numbers may not sum precisely because of rounding.
Sources: ADB. Projects & Tenders. https://www.adb.org/projects (accessed 21 October 2021); and authors' estimates.

Appendix 1, Table A4.2 shows estimated direct job creation from ADB investment projects in Thailand. Direct job creation is defined as the sum of total reported jobs during construction and operations, and the estimated direct domestic purchases. During 2010–2019, 80,603 FTEs were generated, of which 29,301 were female. ADB financing supported the creation of 20,401 FTEs (6,951 female). This was equivalent to about 1,488 jobs per year (460 female).

The model estimates a higher number of total direct jobs created than what has been reported (i.e., 27,667 FTEs) in project documents. The difference is due to the inclusion of direct jobs created from domestic purchases of non-construction goods for the project (other non-intermediate, capital goods) in the model.

The estimates of indirect and induced jobs created as a result of ADB operations are provided in Appendix 1, Table A4.3. It is estimated that 69,428 (25,520 female) indirect jobs have been created from domestic goods purchases during construction and operation of the projects. In addition, 25,058 "induced" jobs (9,566 female), have been created as a result of the spending effect from the workers employed for construction and operation of the asset. Thus, it is estimated that a total of 175,089 jobs were created during 2010–2019 in Thailand, including 64,387 female FTEs.

The indirect and induced jobs were also estimated by using the corresponding employment multipliers from reported direct jobs and estimates generated by the model using the value of all domestic purchases by projects. These direct jobs by sector are then multiplied by Type I and Type II employment multipliers to derive indirect and induced impacts (a sample of employment multipliers in 2019 is given in Appendix 5).

The Eastern Economic Corridor Independent Power Project approved in 2019 was reported to have generated 3,200 direct jobs during project construction. Using employment multipliers for the construction sector in 2019, potentially 4,768 jobs were generated, including 1,088 indirect jobs and 480 induced jobs.[15] In addition, the estimated $514 million local purchase (assumed to be spent on non-construction capital goods and services purchase) follows the pattern of the IO model that would indicate an additional 17,823 total job creation, 7,520 of which are direct jobs, 8,550 are indirect, and 1,753 are induced jobs. The total job creation from this project is 22,591 FTEs, which is the sum of total job creation from both construction and non-construction domestic purchases.

Taking into account the ADB share of total project financing and the construction period, 48,817 jobs (including 16,381 female FTEs) or an average of 3,058 jobs per year (926 female FTEs) would have been created with ADB financing, as estimated with the IO model.

Table 11 shows what ADB operations would have contributed to total job creation per year through direct, indirect, and induced effects, given the sectors they supported. The induced effects would have accounted for 17% (29.8% female), 44.1% would have been through indirect jobs (29.9% female), and 38.9% through direct job creation (30.9% female). Female employment would have accounted for 30.3% of total job creation.

Table 11: Estimate of Annualized Total Job Creation by Sector from ADB-Funded Projects in Thailand, 2010–2019

Sector	Direct		Indirect		Induced		Total	
	All	Female	All	Female	All	Female	All	Female
Construction	596	93	229	36	140	22	966	150
Energy	165	34	627	124	233	46	1,024	204
Transport	18	3	41	7	8	1	68	12
Others	411	238	452	236	138	85	1,001	559
Average	**1,190**	**368**	**1,349**	**403**	**519**	**154**	**3,058**	**926**
	38.9% of Total	*30.9% of all direct*	*44.1% of Total*	*29.9% of all indirect*	*17.0% of Total*	*29.8% of all induced*	*100%*	*30.3% of all*

ADB = Asian Development Bank.
Note: Numbers may not sum precisely because of rounding.
Sources: ADB. Projects & Tenders. https://www.adb.org/projects (accessed 20 October 2021); and authors' estimates.

Results show that the share of direct job creation among all jobs created was relatively small in Thailand. This was partially due to the capital-intensive nature of energy and transport construction projects in Thailand. Indirect and induced effects of ADB operations were larger in comparison, comprising more than 61% of total jobs per annum during 2010–2019.

---

[15] If employment multipliers are used for the construction sector in 2019, potentially 4,768 jobs have been generated, i.e., 3,200 x 1.49 (Type II multiplier). This includes 1,088 indirect jobs, i.e., (4,288 (3,200 x 1.34 (Type I))-3,200), and 480 jobs created due to induced effects, i.e., 4,768–4,288.

Key takeaways from this analysis are the following: (i) the impact of ADB operations on job creation has been underreported over the last decade in Thailand, with project reports focusing mostly on direct effects; (ii) it is important not to overlook indirect and induced jobs when assessing potential job creation through ADB investment projects; and (iii) attribution and annualized estimates would be useful for monitoring, reporting, and evaluation purposes at the sector, country, and ADB corporate levels.

Measuring Jobs Impact of Policy-Based Loans

ADB development assistance delivered through programmatic or budgetary support—where results indicators are not explicitly tagged to job creation—has not been taken into account during corporate results monitoring as of 2022. Policy-based loans comprise a sizable part of the ADB portfolio and can leverage substantial changes in economic outcomes, including through job creation. This section explores possible approaches to addressing this gap in analysis.

Policy-based lending (PBL) is ADB "budget support in conjunction with structural reforms and development programs of a developing member country" (Horridge et al. 2016). There are several PBL variants to respond to different country needs (such as stand-alone, program cluster, Countercyclical Support Facility (CSF) lending, and special policy-based lending). Special policy-based lending and CSF are crisis response instruments. In addition, PBL and investment loans can be combined into sector development programs. The CSF was established in 2009 and mainstreamed in 2011 and its access criteria were refined in 2016 (Asquith 2017). A new modality under the CSF—the coronavirus disease (COVID-19) pandemic response option—was introduced in 2020.

The monitoring and measurement of the development outcome are dependent on the design and monitoring framework and the policy matrix for monitoring and assessing the results of PBL. Assessing the outcome of ADB support for policy reforms is not straightforward as their development outcome might not emerge for some time (ADB 2018b).

The difficulty in assessing the job creation impact of PBLs stems from the high-level—or macro-level—planning nature of a PBL design and monitoring framework. Since they support policy and system reforms, not all PBLs include quantifiable outcomes and do not always produce discrete outputs that are reasonably attributable to the program (ADB 2020c). According to ADB guidelines, when policy-based operations are earmarked to help deliver specific results framework indicators, then the method of calculation must be provided as a linked project document during processing (ADB 2013b).

This option was explored for the COVID-19 Active Response and Expenditure Support Program to Indonesia (ADB 2020b). In response to the crisis, the Government of Indonesia has taken significant fiscal measures, announcing a $32.4 billion package for urgently needed health care, social assistance, and economic support measures (Table 12). ADB lent its support to the Indonesian COVID-19 response and recovery efforts with the $1.5 billion COVID-19 Active Response and Expenditure Support Program, comprising public expenditure and fiscal management ($750 million), social protection ($500 million), and health ($250 million) sector support measures.

The potential impact of the stimulus package on the economy can be estimated using the information in Table 12 and the 2019 IO model developed for Indonesia in this study, with the following inputs into the model (rounded):

(i)   government spending of $4.51 billion,
(ii)   transfers to individuals and tax cuts of $7.04 billion, and
(iii) tax cuts and other support to businesses of $20.88 billion are assumed to be used by all industries to sustain their production by their respective share in the total output.

Table 12: Indonesia's Stimulus Package—Potential Multiplier Effects
($ million)

	COVID-19 Fiscal Package	Overall Fiscal Impact after 1 Year	Overall Fiscal Impact after 2 Years
Government Spending	4,509	6,493	7,079
Transfers to individuals	6,548	9,429	10,280
Transfers to LGU	–	–	–
Tax cuts (indirect tax)	4,618	3,002	4,572
Tax cuts (individual)	491	319	346
Tax cuts (corporate)	1,394	906	1,380
Financial relief	349	349[a]	–
Other expansion of tax incentives	4,000	2,600	3,960
National Recovery Program for businesses and MSMEs	8,571	12,342	13,456[b]
Reserve Fund	1,949	2,807	3,060[b]
Total	**32,429**	**38,245**	**44,482**
As % of 2019 GDP[c]	2.7%	3.2%	3.7%

– = data not available, COVID-19 = coronavirus disease, GDP = gross domestic product, INO = Indonesia, LGU = local government unit, MSME = micro, small, and medium-sized enterprises.
Note: Numbers may not sum precisely because of rounding.
[a] Assume multiplier of 1.
[b] Assume government spending multipliers of 1.4 and 1.57 for first and second years.
[c] Nominal GDP of Indonesia in 2019 was $1.192 trillion.
Source: ADB. 2020. *Estimating the Overall Fiscal Impact of Indonesia and The Philippines COVID-19 Response*. Manila.

Preliminary estimates by ADB using fiscal multipliers from economic literature show that the overall impact of the $32.4 billion fiscal package (2.7% of GDP) could lead to a cumulative increase in real GDP of $38.2 billion after 1 year—equivalent to 3.2% of GDP—and $44.4 billion after 2 years—equivalent to 3.7% of GDP—(Table 13; ADB 2020b). Using the IO model, the total impact of the stimulus package on GDP is estimated to be 2.6%. The difference in results is due to leakages (imports) of household and government expenditure, and the IO model accounts for only the final demand for domestic goods and services.

The model suggests that the stimulus package could retain or save about 3.8 million jobs of the estimated 5.2 million jobs lost due to COVID-19. The impact on female employment would have been fairly significant at around 38% of all jobs created for women.

Since ADB contributed about $1.5 billion—or 5%—of the total stimulus package, results could be attributed using the same percentages (Table 13).

Table 13: Indonesia's Stimulus Package—Potential Impact on Jobs

	GDP ($ billion)				
	Direct	Indirect	Induced	Total	ADB
Government Expenditure	2.776	1.310	0.501	4.587	1.017
Support to Household	3.567	2.354	0.523	6.444	0.458
Support to Firms	10.811	7.573	1.473	19.857	–
Total	**17.154**	**11.237**	**2.497**	**30.888**	**1.475**
% of 2019	*1.4%*	*0.9%*	*0.2%*	*2.6%*	*0.1%*
	Employment				
	Direct	Indirect	Induced	Total	ADB
Government Expenditure	382,170	155,365	67,197	604,732	134,117
Female	166,251	60,373	26,678	253,302	56,177
Support to Household	467,425	326,999	70,114	864,539	61,411
Female	196,274	119,126	27,837	343,238	24,381
Support to Firms	1,279,913	885,819	197,665	2,363,396	–
Female	480,094	318,336	78,477	876,907	–
Total	**2,129,508**	**1,368,183**	**334,976**	**3,832,667**	**195,527**
Female	842,619	497,836	132,992	1,473,447	80,558
% of Total	39.6%	36.4%	39.7%	38.4%	39.6%
% Total of 2019	*1.7%*	*1.1%*	*0.3%*	*3.0%*	*0.2%*

– = data not available, ADB = Asian Development Bank, GDP = gross domestic product.
Note: Numbers may not sum precisely because of rounding.
Source: Authors' estimates.

In summary, the answer is yes. While the methodology would benefit from more complete data during ex ante and ex post assessments, the model can help with understanding the employment impact of PBLs.

Computable General Equilibrium Model

To check the reliability of the results attained with the IO Model, the Global Trade Analysis Project (GTAP) model documented in Corong (2017) was applied, and the job creation impact of selected ADB projects was estimated, chosen from the three country portfolios where the IO model had been applied. The GTAP model is calibrated, based on data from the GTAP version 10 database (Aquita et al. 2019). The model is static and multi-market, with markets for final goods, intermediate goods, traded goods, and factors of production included. It is also multiregional, with a region representing a country or a group of countries. In the computable general equilibrium (CGE) model, it is assumed that there is perfect competition and that prices will adjust to clear all markets. The latest GTAP model —based on the 2014 database—includes Indonesia and Thailand data but not Fiji. For Fiji, the University of the South Pacific-Fiji CGE model was relied on with the IO table at the base year 2015, which is constructed based on ORANI, the Australian static CGE model.[16]

The GTAP and USP-Fiji CGE models were used to verify employment impact from selected ADB projects and programs in Fiji, Indonesia, and Thailand portfolios during 2010–2019, and compared the results with the earlier IO model estimates (which use ADB MRIOTs). Results of the estimates are in Table 14. To have comparability of the estimates with the IO model, the short-run closure was adopted for all GTAP and CGE models where the real wage is fixed and employment is endogenous. Capital stock was also assumed to be fixed. All project values were deflated to match the base year of data in GTAP and CGE models, using ADB Key Indicators for 2020 (ADB 2020d).

For Thailand, government spending was assumed to be exogenous in the GTAP model simulations for the $1.15 billion investment under the Eastern Economic Corridor Independent Power Project. Household spending, exports, and imports were therefore endogenous. The total employment impact from the GTAP model was 15,015 FTEs, which was 34.3% lower than the 22,591 jobs estimated by the IO model. The IO model estimated 5,028 jobs were created under the Greater Mekong Subregion Highway Expansion Phase 2 Project, while the estimates attained using the GTAP model were 2,893 FTEs, which was 42.5% lower than the IO model estimate. Similar patterns were observed for other projects assessed (Table 14).

For Indonesia, aggregate investment was assumed to be fixed, with imports and exports endogenously determined government spending increased, household consumption and output expanded with the COVID-19 Active Response and Expenditure Support Program supporting stimulus measures. The total employment impact of the stimulus using the GTAP/CGE model was estimated to be 3,741,533—or 2.96%—of the total employment in 2019. The GTAP/CGE model estimate was about 2.4% lower than the IO model estimate at 3,832,667 jobs. Similarly, the GTAP/CGE model employment estimate for the Integrated Participatory Development and Management of Irrigation Program was 114,456 FTEs—or 5.5%—lower than the IO model estimated level.

---

[16] Main theoretical features of the model can be found in Horridge (2000) and Dixon et al. (1982). The detailed description of the USP-Fiji CGE model is provided by Oum and Singh (2019).

Table 14: Comparison of Employment Impacts Between Input–Output and the Global Trade Analysis Projects and Computable General Equilibrium Models

	Project	Year of Approval	Investment Cost/Interventions	Input–Output Model (1)	CGE/GTAP Model (2)	% Difference between IO and CGE Estimates[a]
A.	**Fiji**					
1	Transport Infrastructure Investment Sector Project (formerly Bridge Replacement Project)	2014	$116.67 million	2,178 jobs	1,800 jobs	17.3%
2	Emergency Assistance for Recovery from Tropical Cyclone Winston	2016	$80 million for reconstruction and $20 million for cash transfer	2,197 jobs	1,739 jobs	20.8%
3	Urban Water Supply and Wastewater Management Investment Program	2016	$405.1 million	9,202 jobs	7,488 jobs	18.6%
B.	**Indonesia**					
4	COVID-19 Active Response and Expenditure Support Program to Indonesia (CARES)	2020	• Government spending $4.51 billion • Transfers to individuals and tax cuts – $7.04 billion • Tax cuts and other supports to business at $20.88 billion	3,832,667 jobs	3,741,533 jobs	2.4%
5	Integrated Participatory Development and Management of Irrigation Program	2017	$1.55 billion	121,117 jobs	114,456 jobs	5.5%
6	Jawa-1 Liquefied Natural Gas-to-Power Project	2018	$1.42 billion • Estimated local purchase at $32 million (ADB share $250 million) • 4,000 direct jobs during construction, 120 during operation	19,639 jobs	103,819 jobs	(428.6%)
7	Sarulla Geothermal Power Generation Project	2013	$1.24 billion • Estimated local purchase at $200 million • 1,624 construction, 100 operation	38,012 jobs	106,341 jobs	(179.8%)
8	Muara Laboh Geothermal Power Project	2016	$570.9 million • Estimated local purchase at $90 million • 1,400 direct jobs during construction, 190 during operation	18,830 jobs	43,288 jobs	(129.9%)

continued on next page

Table 14   *continued*

	Project	Year of Approval	Investment Cost/Interventions	Input–Output Model (1)	CGE/GTAP Model (2)	% Difference between IO and CGE Estimates[a]
9	Tangguh Liquefied Natural Gas Expansion Project	2016	$400 million • Estimated local purchase at $180 million • 7,000 direct jobs during construction, 29 during operation	48,981 jobs	30,254 jobs	13.8%
C.	**Thailand**					
10	Eastern Economic Corridor Independent Power Project	2019	$1.15 billion • Estimated local purchase (non-construction, capital goods) at $514 million • Direct 3,200 jobs during construction, 60 during operation	22,863 jobs	15,015 jobs	34.3%
11	Greater Mekong Subregion Highway Expansion Phase 2 Project	2017	$213.6 million • Estimated local purchase at $94 million • 917 direct jobs	5,028 jobs	2,893 jobs	42.5%
12	Bangchak Solar Power Project	2010	$145 million • Estimated local purchase at $72.24 million • 200 direct jobs during construction, 72 during operation	4,605 jobs	2,347 jobs	49.0%
13	Subyai Wind Power Project	2014	$83 million • Estimated local purchase at $36.8 million • 419 during construction, 47 during operation	2,311 jobs	1,331 jobs	42.4%
14	Ayudhaya Natural Gas Power Project	2012	$1.52 billion • Estimated local purchase at $754 million • 2,920 during construction, 154 during operation	35,943 jobs	23,463 jobs	34.7%

ADB = Asian Development Bank, CGE = computable general equilibrium, COVID-19 = coronavirus disease, GTAP = Global Trade Analysis Project, IO = input–output.

[a] The percentage difference between IO and CGE models' estimates are calculated as [(1-2)/1]*100, where (1) denotes IO estimates and (2) denotes CGE model estimates. A positive number indicates CGE estimate is lower, and a negative number indicates the IO estimate is lower.

Sources: ADB. Projects & Tenders. https://www.adb.org/projects (accessed 20 October 2021); and authors' estimates.

In the Jawa-1 Liquefied Natural Gas–to–Power Project, the reported share of local purchase of non-construction capital goods and services was relatively low (2.3%), resulting in a large discrepancy between the two models. The IO model estimate of employment impact was four times lower than that of the GTAP model, which used the full project cost of $1.4 billion to estimate job creation impact. Similar results were observed for Sarulla Geothermal Power Generation Project and Muara Laboh Geothermal Power Project. The gap was narrower when the reported direct jobs and share of local purchases were relatively higher, as seen in the Tangguh Liquefied Natural Gas Expansion Project.

In the case of Fiji, it was assumed that exports and government spending were fixed, with an increase in investment and household expenditures from the reconstruction and cash transfers of the Emergency Assistance for Recovery from Tropical Cyclone Winston Program. The employment impact from the CGE model estimate was 1,723 jobs, about 21.6% lower than the IO model estimate (2,197 jobs). A similar exercise undertaken for the $405.1 million Urban Water Supply and Wastewater Management Investment Program yielded a $13.8% difference in employment impact estimates between the IO (9,202 jobs) and CGE models (7,932 jobs).

Results from project-level estimates for the three countries suggest that—in most cases—IO models tend to yield higher jobs impact estimates compared to the GTAP/CGE models. However, the difference between the IO and GTAP/CGE model estimates tend to narrow when a project is financially smaller; it targets one specific sector or only a few sectors, with a significant portion of project proceeds allocated to local non-construction purchases; and its direct job creation impact is close to the industry average, as reported by the IO model (Table 14).

The variations in estimation results are partially due to the different IOT structures for GTAP, ADB MRIOTs, and the national tables. Another reason is that each model has its assumptions. By construct, the IO model assumes there are no supply-side constraints and fixed prices. Therefore, there is no substitution effect from demand shocks. The GTAP (global) and Fiji national CGE models allow for supply and demand to adjust according to relative price changes by industries, households, government, and the rest of the world. Decisions are largely based on the price elasticity of products, demand substitution between domestically produced and imported products, and between factors of production based on factor price movements.

During the analyses, it was noted that the IO and CGE models yielded a wider variation in the ADB Thailand portfolio, compared to the other two country portfolios studied. The higher IO model impact estimates for the five projects in Thailand were due to (i) different underlying assumptions and IOTs, (ii) use of direct employment levels in ex ante and ex post targets as reported in project documents, and (iii) a relatively high share of local purchases (of non-construction capital goods and services) under the five projects (Table 14).

When there are no estimates of direct jobs and local purchases in project documents, it is assumed that project investments, aggregate government expenditures, and household consumption follow the IOT determined patterns for that country. In the GTAP/CGE model simulations, industries, households, government, and the rest of the world are allowed to respond to price changes. These are the cases for projects 1–5 in Table 14 where the differences in employment impact estimates using the IO or GTAP/CGE models are relatively smaller. In such cases, it may be more practical to use the IO model, with its less demanding data and modeling requirements, ease of use, and overall less transaction costs for operations teams.

Model choice is dependent on the nature of interventions, skills required to model, and availability of data. As a general rule, the estimates would be more robust if different models produce similar results for the same intervention and the underlying factors for any differences can be conclusively identified, as seen in Table 14.

Alternative Approaches to Measure Jobs Impact

For relatively small investment projects (with regards to the size of the economy and the ADB portfolio in the economy, sector and industry-specific impact analyses), the IO model is more suitable. To ensure the reliability of the estimates, detailed and accurate data at the project level are necessary, especially when constructing impact models by specific industry to account for different cost structures and labor intensities. Jobs impact of an energy plant construction project is different from construction of roads, buildings, and factories. Jobs impact even differs for construction works for the different types of energy sector (solar, wind, geothermal, gas, etc.).

On the other hand, the GTAP/CGE models can be more appealing for counter-factual policy and impact analyses for large project or program interventions such as changes in taxes, trade policies or agreements, technology, macroeconomic aggregates (household consumption, investment levels and policy, and government spending), and substantial external shocks. A more comprehensive intervention that can potentially impact many sectors would be expected to trigger economic and behavioral change; and despite the more complex structure of a CGE, it would be worthwhile to use a CGE model to capture these complex, multi-tier changes directly and indirectly triggered by ADB interventions.

4 Technical Notes for Robust Assessments

Data and Model Application

The IO models can be used to provide preliminary estimates for potential job creation through ADB projects in selected countries despite data gaps and limitations. Overall, nonsovereign and sovereign loans follow different data monitoring and reporting protocols.[17] It will be important to establish a common approach for ADB operations to ensure data comparability, completeness, and integrity.

It is critical to have an accurate account of direct job creation at the project level. The estimation of the indirect and induced effects should be based on detailed costs and purchases during both construction and operation periods. Costs and labor absorption within the same sector may still vary by the type of project and are often different from industry aggregates. Employment per investment cost and output can also vary within a country and a given industry.

As shown in Table 15, a natural gas power plant requires significant capital investment relative to labor during construction, while a solar or wind power plant requires less capital investment and higher employment per unit investment cost. It has been observed that model-generated employment levels for a given industry are much higher than the level of employment reported during operations per investment cost.

The discrepancy between the actual jobs impact and the estimate widens if there is no actual project data to anchor the impact assessments undertaken with IO or CGE models.

This study (like most project documents) does not make a distinction between part-time and full-time, temporary, and permanent employment. Temporary jobs are created during the inception and implementation (construction) phase. Permanent jobs can be the result of operation and maintenance of the facility, new business opportunities, and expansion of government services (education, health services). Full-time, permanent jobs have very different welfare and poverty reduction impacts than part-time, temporary jobs. Hence, it is suggested that results indicators identify the type of employment to be generated, where possible.

---

[17] Data reporting and verification do not follow the same protocols under sovereign and nonsovereign operations. For sovereign operations data are not tracked in real-time, with the majority of results monitoring and reporting done after project completion when there is limited historical data. For nonsovereign operations, project data are self-reported by sponsors, there is no independent validation. Sponsors report only direct jobs generated under the project (based on cash flow and salary statements), and the highest number of jobs held at any given point within a year is reported as the number of jobs created for that year.

Table 15: Construction Workers per Investment Value, Reported, and Estimated Direct Job Creation

Project	Reported Employment/ $1 million of Investment (from RRP)[a]	Reported Direct Job Creation	IO Model Estimated Direct Job[b]
A. Thailand			
1 Bangchak Solar Power Project	1.4	200	1,582
2 Solar Power Project	6.4	1,753	3,229
3 Subyai Wind Power Project	3.0	419	1,032
4 Nong Saeng Natural Gas Power Project	0.8	3,873	20,273
5 Ayudhaya Natural Gas Power Project	1.3	2,920	16,406
6 Greater Mekong Subregion Highway Expansion Phase 2 Project	4.3	917	2,528
B. Indonesia			
1 Sarulla Geothermal Power Generation Project	1.3	1,624	27,171
2 Muara Laboh Geothermal Power Project	2.4	1,400	11,758
3 Jawa-1 Liquefied Natural Gas-to-Power Project	2.8	4,000	27,365
4 Tangguh Liquefied Natural Gas Expansion Project	17.5	7,000	7,740

IO = input–output, RRP = report and recommendation of the President.

[a] Estimated employment per $1 million of output in the construction industry in 2019 (from IO Model) is 55.66 for Thailand and 23.08 for Indonesia.

[b] IO Model estimates include direct jobs from local purchase plus project-reported direct job creation.

Sources: ADB. Projects & Tenders. https://www.adb.org/projects (accessed 20 October 2021); and authors' estimates.

At present, there is insufficient information to estimate the second-order or growth-related jobs that occur throughout the economy through backward and forward linkages; for instance, from the operation and utilization of infrastructure assets created. In most cases, supplementary data on input requirements for operation of plants and potential productivity, or economy-wide cost reduction from new infrastructure assets or new business opportunities, are unavailable.

Furthermore, estimation of employment effects (i.e., net of potential job displacement and substitution effects within and between industries from a given project), is beyond the scope of this study. However, it would be useful to consider job displacement and substitution effects, especially for countries with a labor shortage or tight labor market conditions. One way to address this could be by applying a downward adjustment ratio, as suggested by Kluve and Stöterau (2014). They suggest the lower and upper bound of the adjustment by netting out 10% to 30% of the displacement effect, and 20% to 40% of substitution effect from gross effects. Although their approach is appealing for users to adjust the potential estimation from the IO model, the selection of the range can be problematic as it potentially covers 30% to 70% change. The adjustment ranges can be more accurately selected with adequate empirical evidence from pre and post evaluations.

The impact of policy and program loans on job creation has not been fully captured. PBLs can have a significant employment impact, as they target medium- and longer-term structural issues such as trade, investment and financial sector development, institutional reforms, human capital, innovation, and technology development. As discussed in Section 3.4, it is possible to assess the impact of PBLs, provided transmission channels are clear and potential job creation is tracked throughout the life-cycle of a program, i.e., from design to completion.

Measures to Improve Jobs Impact Assessment

A standard methodology to assess both ex ante and ex post employment impact of ADB operations could help results capture at the corporate level. If IO models are used in the process, detailed sector IO tables—accompanied by employment and wage data—would be needed to ensure consistency and reliability of the estimations.

A standard dataset—accompanied by clear definitions, guidance, and template for operations teams to use in collecting and reporting data—could be included for each project to help assess operational impact systematically. As of 2022, most of these data categories are generated during project implementation through financial statements, periodic (monthly, quarterly, biannual) reports of project sponsors, construction companies, and supervision engineers that track progress. Operations documents that track project or program progress—such as project administration manuals, summary poverty reduction and social strategy documents, and gender action plans—could be valuable conduits for capturing the indicated data and incorporating them in ADB results monitoring workstreams and databases.

Building on good practices of nonsovereign investment projects, sovereign projects could also include direct job creation results indicators. Project administration manuals could be enhanced to capture more real-time data on the quality, nature, and number of jobs created and expenditures (by product and source) during project implementation. Project data collected from project sites and compiled in real time as references for project cost structure and direct employment generation by types of projects and sectors would help generate robust assessments.

Employment data generated by project monitoring systems could then be periodically collated, analyzed, and aggregated, and progress assessed against targets for timely remedial measures and course correction where needed.

To generate reliable results while using the model, it would be important to verify estimates against actual impact, where project data are available. This could be done by validating results with some case studies and checking whether the employment impact captured through these case studies differs significantly from model-generated estimates. The approach can then be further calibrated and enhanced, informed by these "proofs of concept."

Improving data capture and systematic monitoring of ADB operations' impact during design, implementation, and post-implementation periods would further complement quantitative assessments presented in this study, and support poverty reduction impact assessments.

Conclusion 5

There is a wide range of methodologies used by international and bilateral development agencies to estimate the employment impacts of development assistance. In developing an optimized approach relevant for ADB operations, the research team had extensive consultations with internal stakeholders (such as the Private Sector Operations Department; Strategy, Policy, and Partnerships Department; Sustainable Development and Climate Change Department; and the regional departments) and external stakeholders (such as the 18 members of the Multilateral Development Banks Managing for Development Results Group). Preliminary results were shared with ADB resident missions and country teams in Fiji, Indonesia, and Thailand, and within the Economic Research and Regional Cooperation Department to further refine the methodology developed in consultation with development partners and potential future users of the model.

This study summarizes the methodology developed to assess the impact of ADB operations on creating jobs. In developing a methodology that can be readily applied to ADB operations, the starting point was the IO model, which was used to estimate the impact of ADB interventions on indirect and induced employment. The jobs impact estimates derived by using the IO model were compared to (i) actual jobs reported under ADB operations in three pilot countries, i.e., Fiji, Indonesia, and Thailand during 2010–2019; and (ii) jobs impact estimates generated with GTAP/CGE models.

It is difficult to declare a single model as universally superior across all use cases. As a general rule, the estimates would be more robust if different models produce similar results for the same intervention and the sources of differences can be identified. Moving forward, the choice of model will likely depend on the nature of the interventions, user preferences, and availability of data.

Findings suggest that for investment projects, sector, and industry-specific impact analyses where there is a substantial local purchase component, the IO model is more suitable. However, to ensure the reliability of the estimates, detailed and accurate project-level data are necessary, especially for construction by specific industries to account for different cost structures and employment intensity. The GTAP/CGE models can be more appealing for counter-factual policy and impact analyses such as changes in taxes, trades, technology, macroeconomic aggregates (household, investment, and government spending), and external shocks. Under either approach, the results from ex ante estimates must be compared with actual impact during ex post project impact assessments, where data are available. Any gaps or differences in results can then be used as credible references for remedial adjustments in future applications of this approach.

While this was outside the scope of this study, it would be useful to undertake real-time pilot testing of the model with projects that are under implementation and in design phase. A hybrid approach can be adopted in future studies, that would balance the technical complexity of the model to be used with the financial and economic footprint of the intervention and robustness of estimates that can be attained with the model. To validate and track the potential and actual jobs impact of ongoing and pipeline projects, one project from each piloted country could be selected to further test and refine the model. The results could then help assess and enhance ADB's operational effectiveness (where effectiveness is measured by the number of jobs created), and inform policy measures and investment decisions of ADB members.

Jobs Impact Estimates

Table A1.1: The 35-Sector ADB Multi-Regional Input–Output Database

1	Agriculture, hunting, forestry, and fishing
2	Mining and quarrying
3	Food, beverages, and tobacco
4	Textiles and textile products
5	Leather, leather products, and footwear
6	Wood and products of wood and cork
7	Pulp, paper, paper products, printing, and publishing
8	Coke, refined petroleum, and nuclear fuel
9	Chemicals and chemical products
10	Rubber and plastics
11	Other nonmetallic minerals
12	Basic metals and fabricated metal
13	Machinery, nec
14	Electrical and optical equipment
15	Transport equipment
16	Manufacturing, nec; recycling
17	Electricity, gas, and water supply
18	Construction
19	Sale, maintenance, and repair of motor vehicles and motorcycles; retail sale of fuel
20	Wholesale trade and commission trade, except of motor vehicles and motorcycles
21	Retail trade, except of motor vehicles and motorcycles; repair of household goods
22	Hotels and restaurants
23	Inland transport
24	Water transport
25	Air transport
26	Other supporting and auxiliary transport activities; activities of travel agencies
27	Post and telecommunications
28	Financial intermediation
29	Real estate activities
30	Renting of M&Eq and other business activities
31	Public administration and defense; compulsory social security
32	Education
33	Health and social work
34	Other community, social, and personal services
35	Private households with employed persons

ADB = Asian Development Bank, M&Eq = machinery and equipment, nec = not elsewhere classified.

Source: ADB. Multi-Regional Input–Output Database. https://data.adb.org/taxonomy/term/476 (accessed 20 October 2021).

Table A1.2: Estimates of Direct Job Creation from Investment Projects in Fiji, 2010–2019
(full-time equivalent)

Year	Construction		Others		Total	
	All	Female	All	Female	All	Female
A. Total Projects						
2010	973	33	422	158	1,395	191
2014	1,362	499	303	68	1,664	568
2015	125	45	37	45	162	53
2016	6,180	2,173	2,269	2,755	8,447	2,667
Total	**8,640**	**2,751**	**3,031**	**3,026**	**11,669**	**3,479**
B. Attribution to ADB						
2010	567	19	246	92	813	112
2014	1,167	428	260	59	1,427	486
2015	35	13	10	13	46	15
2016	2,459	865	930	1,130	3,387	1,069
Total	**4,229**	**1,325**	**1,446**	**1,293**	**5,673**	**1,682**
C. Attribution to ADB (Annualized)						
2010	142	5	61	23	203	28
2014	1	0	31	10	82	14
2015	9	3	3	3	11	4
2016	347	122	156	191	502	158
Average	**125**	**33**	**63**	**57**	**200**	**51**

ADB = Asian Development Bank.
Note: Numbers may not sum precisely because of rounding.
Sources: ADB. Projects & Tenders. https://www.adb.org/projects (accessed 20 October 2021); and authors' estimates.

Table A1.3: Estimates of Potential Economy-wide Job Creation from Investment Projects in Fiji, 2010–2019
(full-time equivalent)

Year	Direct		Indirect		Induced		Total	
	All	Female	All	Female	All	Female	All	Female
A. Total Projects								
2010	1,395	191	477	151	117	36	1,989	378
2014	1,664	568	452	140	61	20	2,178	727
2015	162	53	49	14	8	2	220	69
2016	8,447	2,667	2,534	708	418	119	11,399	3,494
Total	**11,669**	**3,479**	**3,513**	**1,013**	**603**	**177**	**15,785**	**4,669**
B. Attribution to ADB								
2010	813	112	278	88	68	21	1,159	220
2014	1,427	486	388	120	52	17	1,866	624
2015	46	15	14	4	2	1	62	20
2016	3,387	1,069	1,018	284	169	48	4,574	1,401
Total	**5,673**	**1,682**	**1,698**	**496**	**291**	**87**	**7,662**	**2,265**
C. Attribution to ADB (Annualized)								
2010	203	28	69	22	17	5	290	55
2014	82	14	36	9	5	2	123	24
2015	11	4	3	1	1	0	16	5
2016	502	158	153	42	26	7	681	208
Average	**200**	**51**	**66**	**18**	**12**	**4**	**278**	**73**

ADB = Asian Development Bank.
Note: Numbers may not sum precisely because of rounding.
Sources: ADB. Project Database. https://www.adb.org/projects (accessed 20 October 2021); and authors' estimates.

Table A1.4: Estimates of Direct Job Creation from Investment Projects in Indonesia, 2010–2019
(full-time equivalent)

Year	Construction All	Construction NS	Construction F	Energy All	Energy NS	Energy F	Transport All	Transport NS	Transport F	Others All	Others NS	Others F	Total All	Total NS	Total F
A. Total Projects															
2010	3,300	–	82	–	–	–	89	–	8	3,608	–	1,344	6,997	–	1,433
2011	9,278	–	240	–	–	–	214	–	15	9,419	–	3,493	18,911	–	3,748
2012	2,997	–	66	–	–	–	56	–	3	2,979	–	1,099	6,032	–	1,168
2013	12,324	1,624	308	100	100	16	717	519	44	34,440	24,927	12,605	47,581	27,171	12,972
2014	9,352	70	237	–	–	–	174	25	11	8,409	1,222	3,077	17,935	1,318	3,325
2015	13,630	–	320	–	–	–	153	–	10	7,966	–	2,956	21,749	–	3,286
2016	15,478	8,400	364	219	219	37	710	597	47	35,604	29,908	13,034	52,011	39,123	13,483
2017	64,643	500	1,422	50	50	9	943	69	63	62,959	4,632	22,986	128,595	5,252	24,479
2018	10,163	5,000	220	220	220	38	554	501	38	32,721	30,026	13,394	43,658	35,748	13,689
2019	8,577	–	185	–	–	–	78	–	5	3,905	–	1,443	12,560	–	1,634
Total	**149,743**	**15,594**	**3,443**	**589**	**589**	**100**	**3,688**	**1,712**	**245**	**202,009**	**90,716**	**75,430**	**356,029**	**108,611**	**79,218**
B. Attribution to ADB															
2010	1,705	–	42	–	–	–	46	–	4	1,864	–	694	3,616	–	741
2011	5,407	–	140	–	–	–	125	–	9	5,489	–	2,036	11,020	–	2,184
2012	2,609	–	57	–	–	–	49	–	3	2,593	–	956	5,250	–	1,016
2013	6,970	433	174	27	27	4	259	138	16	12,451	6,639	4,557	19,707	7,237	4,751
2014	3,548	70	90	–	–	–	81	25	5	3,915	1,222	1,433	7,544	1,318	1,528
2015	13,062	–	307	–	–	–	147	–	9	7,635	–	2,833	20,843	–	3,149
2016	12,672	7,148	298	49	–	8	508	419	34	25,440	21,043	9,313	38,669	28,611	9,654
2017	21,102	233	464	23	–	4	317	32	21	21,137	2,184	7,717	42,579	2,450	8,206
2018	4,832	958	105	46	–	8	160	120	11	8,437	6,462	3,195	13,476	7,540	3,318
2019	7,123	–	154	–	–	–	65	–	4	3,243	–	1,198	10,431	–	1,357
Total	**79,030**	**8,842**	**1,831**	**145**	**27**	**25**	**1,755**	**735**	**117**	**92,204**	**37,551**	**33,932**	**173,134**	**47,154**	**35,904**
C. Attribution to ADB (Annualized)															
2010	405	–	10	–	–	–	11	–	1	442	–	165	858	–	176
2011	883	–	23	–	–	–	20	–	1	896	–	332	1,799	–	357
2012	409	–	9	–	–	–	8	–	0	406	–	150	822	–	159
2013	1,159	108	29	27	27	4	54	35	3	2,594	1,660	949	3,833	1,829	986
2014	550	70	14	–	–	–	33	25	2	1,594	1,222	583	2,176	1,318	599
2015	3,265	–	77	–	–	–	37	–	2	1,909	–	708	5,211	–	787
2016	4,705	3,574	111	49	49	8	228	209	15	11,407	10,497	4,176	16,388	14,330	4,310
2017	3,974	117	87	23	23	4	69	16	5	4,588	1,080	1,675	8,654	1,237	1,771
2018	1,136	361	25	46	46	8	66	58	4	3,626	3,222	1,414	4,874	3,687	1,451
2019	1,696	–	37	–	–	–	15	–	1	772	–	285	2,484	–	323
Average	**1,818**	**423**	**42**	**15**	**15**	**2**	**54**	**34**	**4**	**2,823**	**1,768**	**1,044**	**4,710**	**2,240**	**1,092**

– = data not available; ADB = Asian Development Bank; F = of which, female; NS = of which, nonsovereign.

Note: Numbers may not sum precisely because of rounding.

Sources: ADB. Projects & Tenders. https://www.adb.org/projects (accessed 20 October 2021); and authors' estimates.

Table A1.5: Estimates of Potential Economy-wide Job Creation from Investment Projects in Indonesia, 2010–2019
(full-time equivalent)

Year	Direct			Indirect			Induced			Total		
	All	NS	F	All	NS	F	All	NS	F	All	NS	F
A. Total Projects												
2010	6,997	–	1,433	7,540	–	2,662	1,014	–	385	15,551	–	4,480
2011	18,911	–	3,748	18,453	–	6,368	2,601	–	998	39,965	–	11,114
2012	6,032	–	1,168	5,637	–	1,947	861	–	331	12,530	–	3,445
2013	47,581	27,171	12,972	28,598	8,700	8,990	4,962	2,142	1,770	81,141	38,012	23,732
2014	17,935	1,318	3,325	15,548	378	5,241	1,954	86	746	35,437	1,782	9,313
2015	21,749	–	3,286	25,496	–	8,809	2,857	–	1,104	50,102	–	13,200
2016	52,011	39,123	13,483	38,765	24,272	8,537	6,481	4,416	1,811	97,257	67,812	23,831
2017	128,595	5,252	24,479	122,302	1,956	43,160	20,657	325	8,109	271,554	7,533	75,749
2018	43,658	35,748	13,689	33,423	21,297	9,182	8,052	5,862	2,757	85,132	62,907	25,628
2019	12,560	–	1,634	20,569	–	7,311	3,119	–	1,238	36,248	–	10,183
Total	**356,029**	**108,611**	**79,218**	**316,329**	**56,604**	**102,206**	**52,558**	**12,831**	**19,250**	**724,917**	**178,046**	**200,674**
B. Attribution to ADB												
2010	3,616	–	741	3,896	–	1,375	524	–	199	8,035	–	2,315
2011	11,020	–	2,184	10,753	–	3,711	1,516	–	581	23,289	–	6,476
2012	5,250	–	1,016	4,906	–	1,694	749	–	288	10,906	–	2,999
2013	19,707	7,237	4,751	14,474	2,317	4,761	2,293	571	842	36,474	10,124	10,355
2014	7,544	1,318	1,528	6,062	378	2,025	786	86	298	14,392	1,782	3,851
2015	20,843	–	3,149	24,433	–	8,442	2,738	–	1,058	48,015	–	12,650
2016	38,669	28,611	9,654	30,336	19,025	6,397	4,952	3,340	1,334	73,956	50,976	17,384
2017	42,579	2,450	8,206	40,067	913	14,098	6,767	152	2,655	89,412	3,514	24,959
2018	13,476	7,540	3,318	13,058	3,959	3,988	2,775	1,132	979	29,308	12,630	8,285
2019	10,431	–	1,357	17,082	–	6,071	2,590	–	1,028	30,102	–	8,456
Total	**173,134**	**47,154**	**35,904**	**165,067**	**26,592**	**52,563**	**25,690**	**5,280**	**9,263**	**363,890**	**79,026**	**97,730**
C. Attribution to ADB (Annualized)												
2010	858	–	176	924	–	326	124	–	47	1,906	–	549
2011	1,799	–	357	1,756	–	606	247	–	95	3,802	–	1,057
2012	822	–	159	768	–	265	117	–	45	1,708	–	470
2013	3,833	1,829	986	2,591	638	825	428	151	153	6,852	2,618	1,964
2014	2,176	1,318	599	1,162	378	364	182	86	66	3,521	1,782	1,030
2015	5,211	–	787	6,108	–	2,111	685	–	265	12,004	–	3,162
2016	16,388	14,330	4,310	11,897	9,582	2,034	2,010	1,680	483	30,295	25,592	6,827
2017	8,654	1,237	1,771	7,722	485	2,669	1,349	126	517	17,725	1,847	4,957
2018	4,874	3,687	1,451	3,644	1,824	1,075	877	548	309	9,395	6,060	2,835
2019	2,484	–	323	4,067	–	1,446	617	–	245	7,167	–	2,013
Average	**4,710**	**4,480**	**1,092**	**4,064**	**2,581**	**1,172**	**664**	**518**	**222**	**9,438**	**7,580**	**2,486**

– = data not available; ADB = Asian Development Bank; F = of which, female; NS = of which, nonsovereign.
Note: Numbers may not sum precisely because of rounding.
Sources: ADB. Projects & Tenders. https://www.adb.org/projects (accessed 20 October 2021); and authors' estimates.

Table A1.6: Estimates of Direct Job Creation
from Investment Projects in Thailand, 2010–2019
(full-time equivalent)

Year	Construction All	Construction F	Energy All	Energy F	Transport All	Transport F	Others All	Others F	Total All	Total F
A. Total Projects										
2010	1,953	306	954	182	35	6	1,869	856	4,811	1,351
2011	3,873	601	90	22	305	51	16,005	7,351	20,273	8,026
2012	3,187	555	247	59	253	49	13,677	6,403	17,364	7,066
2013	1,255	205	66	16	12	2	632	295	1,965	519
2014	279	43	47	12	14	3	692	316	1,032	374
2017	1,217	175	65	19	45	9	1,812	818	3,139	1,021
2018	5,476	834	–	–	321	62	10,631	4,825	16,428	5,720
2019	5,860	867	115	34	218	42	9,398	4,281	15,592	5,224
Total	**23,100**	**3,586**	**1,584**	**345**	**1,202**	**224**	**54,716**	**25,147**	**80,603**	**29,301**
B. Attribution to ADB										
2010	1,953	306	954	182	35	6	1,869	856	4,811	1,351
2011	411	64	10	2	32	5	1,697	779	2,149	851
2012	430	75	33	8	26	5	1,407	659	1,896	746
2013	760	124	40	10	7	1	383	179	1,190	314
2014	178	27	30	8	9	2	442	202	659	239
2017	731	105	65	19	24	5	979	442	1,799	571
2018	1,102	168	–	–	132	25	4,596	2,086	5,829	2,279
2019	1,082	160	21	6	22	4	943	429	2,068	600
Total	**6,646**	**1,029**	**1,153**	**235**	**287**	**54**	**12,314**	**5,632**	**20,401**	**6,951**
C. Attribution to ADB (Annualized)										
2010	1,953	306	954	182	35	6	1,869	856	4,811	1,351
2011	137	21	10	2	11	2	566	260	723	285
2012	209	36	33	8	10	2	516	241	767	288
2013	760	124	40	10	7	1	383	179	1,190	314
2014	178	27	30	8	4	1	221	101	434	137
2017	208	30	65	19	3	1	122	55	398	104
2018	356	54	–	–	41	8	617	278	1,014	341
2019	971	144	21	6	8	2	310	140	1,310	292
Average	**596**	**93**	**165**	**34**	**18**	**3**	**729**	**334**	**1,488**	**460**

– = data not available, ADB = Asian Development Bank, F = female.

Note: Numbers may not sum precisely because of rounding.

Sources: ADB. Projects & Tenders. https://www.adb.org/projects (accessed 20 October 2021); and authors' estimates.

Table A1.7: Estimates of Potential Economy-wide Job Creation
from Investment Projects in Thailand, 2010–2019
(full-time equivalent)

Year	Direct		Indirect		Induced		Total	
	All	Female	All	Female	All	Female	All	Female
A. Total Projects								
2010	4,811	1,351	8,009	2,054	3,281	866	16,101	4,271
2011	20,273	8,026	15,085	5,902	7,117	2,998	42,475	16,926
2012	17,364	7,066	14,361	5,758	6,368	2,686	38,093	15,511
2013	1,965	519	1,054	344	616	183	3,635	1,046
2014	1,032	374	884	331	395	149	2,311	854
2017	3,139	1,021	2,487	897	628	224	6,253	2,142
2018	16,428	5,720	14,296	5,346	3,453	1,300	34,177	12,367
2019	15,592	5,224	13,252	4,887	3,200	1,159	32,044	11,270
Total	**80,603**	**29,301**	**69,428**	**25,520**	**25,058**	**9,566**	**175,089**	**64,387**
B. Attribution to ADB								
2010	4,811	1,351	8,009	2,054	3,281	866	16,101	4,271
2011	2,149	851	1,599	626	755	318	4,503	1,794
2012	1,896	746	1,516	600	684	282	4,095	1,628
2013	1,190	314	638	208	373	111	2,201	633
2014	659	239	565	211	252	95	1,476	546
2017	1,799	571	1,425	505	365	127	3,589	1,203
2018	5,829	2,279	5,734	2,243	1,294	532	12,858	5,054
2019	2,068	600	1,525	523	402	129	3,995	1,252
Total	**20,401**	**6,951**	**21,011**	**6,971**	**7,405**	**2,459**	**48,817**	**16,381**
C. Attribution to ADB (Annualized)								
2010	4,811	1,351	8,009	2,054	3,281	866	16,101	4,271
2011	723	285	545	211	257	107	1,525	604
2012	767	288	609	232	281	110	1,658	630
2013	1,190	314	638	208	373	111	2,201	633
2014	434	137	336	117	163	55	932	309
2017	544	170	480	164	124	42	1,149	375
2018	1,740	668	1,680	652	385	155	3,804	1,475
2019	1,696	466	1,190	395	324	99	3,210	961
Average	**1,190**	**368**	**1,349**	**403**	**519**	**154**	**3,058**	**926**

ADB = Asian Development Bank.

Note: Numbers may not sum precisely because of rounding.

Sources: ADB. Projects & Tenders. https://www.adb.org/projects (accessed 20 October 2021); and authors' estimates.

APPENDIX 2
Fiji

Table A2.1: Labor Compensation in the Input–Output Table for Fiji
($ million)

		2010	2011	2012	2013	2014	2015	2016	2017	2018	2019
1	Agriculture, hunting, forestry, and fishing	40.9	46.9	57.6	59.7	54.8	52.6	64.5	73.4	73.6	76.4
2	Mining and quarrying	20.9	24.0	27.0	24.4	18.5	18.9	19.0	19.0	15.8	14.8
3	Food, beverages, and tobacco	51.8	59.4	59.9	58.2	58.2	58.9	58.3	59.8	58.9	59.5
4	Textiles and textile products	10.7	12.1	12.3	11.9	12.0	11.7	12.2	12.5	12.4	12.5
5	Leather, leather products, and footwear	1.2	1.4	1.4	1.4	1.4	1.4	1.4	1.4	1.4	1.4
6	Wood and products of wood and cork	5.3	5.9	5.9	5.8	5.8	5.8	5.8	5.9	4.9	5.0
7	Paper products, printing, and publishing	6.2	7.3	7.4	7.3	7.2	7.3	7.1	7.3	7.5	7.6
8	Coke, refined petroleum, and nuclear fuel	0.1	0.2	0.2	0.2	–	–	–	–	–	–
9	Chemicals and chemical products	5.2	5.9	6.0	5.8	6.1	5.9	5.9	6.1	6.1	6.2
10	Rubber and plastics	1.6	1.8	1.9	1.9	1.8	1.8	1.9	1.9	2.2	2.2
11	Other nonmetallic minerals	3.2	3.6	3.6	3.5	3.5	3.5	3.5	3.6	3.3	3.3
12	Basic metals and fabricated metal	7.6	8.8	8.8	8.7	8.6	8.7	8.7	8.9	7.6	7.7
13	Machinery, nec	1.0	1.2	1.2	1.1	1.1	1.1	1.1	1.2	1.3	1.3
14	Electrical and optical equipment	0.0	0.0	0.0	0.0	0.0	0.0	0.0	0.0	–	–
15	Transport equipment	0.5	0.6	0.6	0.6	0.6	0.5	0.6	0.6	0.5	0.5
16	Manufacturing, nec; recycling	6.4	7.3	7.4	7.1	7.2	7.2	7.2	7.4	7.3	7.4
17	Electricity, gas, and water supply	18.0	20.6	22.1	20.7	20.7	21.3	24.4	27.0	30.6	32.7
18	Construction	32.9	37.7	29.4	30.5	30.7	29.6	31.4	34.5	35.5	36.1
19	Sale and maintenance	1.7	2.0	2.1	59.6	2.0	2.1	2.3	2.7	2.6	2.6
20	Wholesale trade	65.1	74.6	79.2	18.9	76.3	83.0	88.6	102.8	95.9	96.5
21	Retail trade	30.9	35.4	37.6	36.1	36.2	38.0	41.1	47.7	43.9	44.1
22	Hotels and restaurants	82.8	94.9	99.3	99.9	104.4	101.6	104.0	113.4	115.2	119.6
23	Inland transport	13.5	15.5	17.4	15.0	18.3	21.6	23.7	26.6	27.0	26.4
24	Water transport	6.4	7.3	8.1	0.0	8.7	9.1	9.6	10.6	9.1	8.8
25	Air transport	45.4	52.1	57.8	7.4	62.5	63.5	63.9	71.6	62.7	60.2
26	Other transport services	25.4	29.1	33.1	94.5	34.3	35.9	37.7	42.2	43.3	41.6
27	Post and telecommunications	31.9	36.6	44.1	41.4	41.3	40.1	42.1	41.5	40.7	42.2
28	Financial intermediation	58.8	67.4	68.6	68.2	84.2	79.7	78.3	86.2	83.6	84.9
29	Real estate activities	3.0	3.4	3.7	3.7	3.4	3.4	3.5	3.6	3.6	3.6
30	Renting and other business activities	53.9	61.7	68.6	68.2	74.5	74.1	79.8	88.5	86.5	87.8
31	Public administration and defense	144.6	165.8	179.0	185.2	223.1	228.5	233.3	266.5	262.2	262.6
32	Education	155.6	178.3	193.7	190.1	216.1	214.3	222.8	257.1	248.0	251.9
33	Health and social work	43.9	50.3	53.9	53.6	64.3	64.1	61.6	62.0	63.1	66.1
34	Other services	22.3	25.8	25.3	24.0	18.5	18.3	20.4	21.0	20.6	20.8
35	Private households with employed persons	1.6	1.7	1.6	1.6	–	–	–	–	–	–

– = data not available, nec = not elsewhere classified.

Sources: ADB. Multi-Regional Input–Output Database. https://data.adb.org/taxonomy/term/476 (accessed 20 October 2021; and Fiji Bureau of Statistics. https://www.statsfiji.gov.fj/ (accessed 20 October 2021).

Table A2.2: Employment in the Input–Output Table for Fiji
(thousand)

		2010	2011	2012	2013	2014	2015	2016	2017	2018	2019
1	Agriculture, hunting, forestry, and fishing	2.20	2.31	2.33	2.36	2.48	5.57	5.65	5.66	5.69	5.94
2	Mining and quarrying	0.88	1.49	1.51	1.53	2.14	1.94	1.97	1.97	2.06	2.00
3	Food, beverages, and tobacco	10.76	10.81	10.92	11.05	10.31	11.05	10.30	11.95	12.63	12.90
4	Textiles and textile products	2.22	2.20	2.24	2.25	2.13	2.19	2.16	2.50	2.65	2.71
5	Leather, leather products, and footwear	0.25	0.25	0.25	0.26	0.24	0.26	0.25	0.29	0.29	0.30
6	Wood and products of wood and cork	1.10	1.07	1.08	1.09	1.02	1.09	1.02	1.18	1.06	1.08
7	Paper products, printing, and publishing	1.30	1.34	1.35	1.38	1.28	1.38	1.26	1.46	1.61	1.64
8	Coke, refined petroleum, and nuclear fuel	0.03	0.04	0.03	0.03	–	–	–	–	–	–
9	Chemicals and chemical products	1.07	1.08	1.09	1.11	1.08	1.11	1.05	1.22	1.31	1.34
10	Rubber and plastics	0.33	0.34	0.34	0.35	0.33	0.35	0.33	0.38	0.46	0.47
11	Other nonmetallic minerals	0.65	0.66	0.66	0.67	0.62	0.67	0.62	0.72	0.71	0.72
12	Basic metals and fabricated metal	1.57	1.59	1.61	1.65	1.53	1.63	1.54	1.78	1.63	1.67
13	Machinery, nec	0.21	0.21	0.21	0.22	0.20	0.21	0.20	0.23	0.27	0.28
14	Electrical and optical equipment	0.00	0.00	0.00	0.00	0.00	0.00	0.00	0.00	–	–
15	Transport equipment	0.10	0.10	0.10	0.11	0.10	0.10	0.10	0.12	0.11	0.12
16	Manufacturing, nec; recycling	1.32	1.33	1.34	1.35	1.28	1.35	1.28	1.48	1.56	1.59
17	Electricity, gas, and water supply	2.08	2.69	2.72	2.75	3.23	3.97	4.00	4.06	3.98	3.97
18	Construction	6.39	6.06	6.13	6.21	11.28	11.49	11.57	11.75	11.80	12.96
19	Sale and maintenance	0.37	0.38	0.38	11.39	0.38	0.50	0.51	0.53	0.54	0.55
20	Wholesale trade	13.79	14.24	14.40	3.62	14.13	19.58	19.48	20.11	20.21	20.78
21	Retail trade	6.55	6.75	6.83	6.90	6.70	8.97	9.03	9.32	9.25	9.51
22	Hotels and restaurants	13.49	13.64	13.79	13.98	13.37	16.80	16.93	17.18	17.59	17.71
23	Inland transport	1.22	1.30	1.31	1.15	1.29	2.18	2.34	2.34	2.55	2.63
24	Water transport	0.57	0.61	0.61	0.00	0.61	0.92	0.95	0.93	0.86	0.87
25	Air transport	4.10	4.36	4.36	0.57	4.40	6.39	6.30	6.32	5.92	6.00
26	Other transport services	2.30	2.44	2.50	7.20	2.41	3.62	3.71	3.72	4.09	4.14
27	Post and telecommunications	2.22	2.69	2.72	2.75	4.63	3.80	3.84	3.88	3.90	3.76
28	Financial intermediation	3.77	3.66	3.70	3.75	5.05	5.18	5.22	5.29	5.30	5.51
29	Real estate activities	1.05	1.09	1.10	1.12	0.51	0.65	0.65	0.66	0.69	0.72
30	Renting and other business activities	9.11	10.26	10.37	10.51	9.99	13.07	13.11	13.41	13.32	13.47
31	Public administration and defense	13.82	13.87	14.02	14.21	15.82	16.81	17.04	17.09	17.19	17.45
32	Education	14.78	15.41	15.58	15.79	16.33	16.06	15.90	16.71	16.74	17.06
33	Health and social work	4.90	5.19	5.25	5.32	5.75	8.25	9.26	7.49	7.49	7.52
34	Other services	1.97	2.03	2.05	2.08	3.26	3.02	3.02	3.11	3.29	3.39
35	Private households with employed persons	0.15	0.13	0.13	0.13	–	–	–	–	–	–

– = data not available, nec = not elsewhere classified.

Sources: ADB. Multi-Regional Input–Output Database. https://data.adb.org/taxonomy/term/476 (accessed 20 October 2021); and Fiji Bureau of Statistics. https://www.statsfiji.gov.fj/ (accessed 20 October 2021).

Table A2.3: Summary of ADB Projects in Fiji, 2010–2019
($ million)

	Project	Approval	Construction and Implementation Period	Total Finance	Financed by ADB
1	Third Road Upgrading (Sector) Project (Supplementary Loan)	2009	2010–2013	72.60	26.80
2	Emergency Flood Recovery (Sector) Project	2009	2011–2014	19.99	17.56
3	Suva-Nausori Water Supply and Sewerage Project (Supplementary Loan)	2009	2010–2013	23.00	23.00
4	Transport Infrastructure Investment Sector Project (formerly Bridge Replacement Project)	2014	2015–2022	116.67	100.00
5	Project Design Advance Urban Water Supply and Wastewater Management Project	2015	2015–2018	9.35	2.65
6	Emergency Assistance for Recovery from Tropical Cyclone Winston	2016	2016–2018	100.00	50.00
7	Urban Water Supply and Wastewater Management Investment Program	2016	2016–2026	405.10	153.00
8	Sustained Private Sector-Led Growth Reform Program (subprogram 1)	2018	2018–2020	30.00	15.00
9	Sustained Private Sector-Led Growth Reform Program (subprogram 2)	2019	2019–2020	130.00	65.00

ADB = Asian Development Bank.

Note: The Third Road Upgrading (Sector) Project (Supplementary Loan), Emergency Flood Recovery (Sector) Project and the Suva-Nausori Water Supply and Sewerage Project (Supplementary Loan) were approved in 2009 but implementation started in 2010. Hence, they are included in the 2010-2019 assessment in this study.

Source: ADB. Projects & Tenders. https://www.adb.org/projects (accessed 20 October 2021).

Indonesia

Table A3.1: Labor Compensation in the Input–Output Table for Indonesia
($ million)

		2010	2011	2012	2013	2014	2015	2016	2017	2018	2019
1	Agriculture, hunting, forestry, and fishing	32,104.2	38,466.0	41,340.2	38,156.3	36,523.7	37,168.9	41,826.1	43,981.3	45,621.3	45,263.2
2	Mining and quarrying	3,124.7	4,512.3	4,829.7	4,880.7	4,296.6	4,002.4	4,257.5	4,563.2	4,928.2	4,832.0
3	Food, beverages, and tobacco	5,936.4	6,855.2	8,280.2	8,075.7	4,460.2	8,913.7	10,522.5	13,143.4	13,961.7	14,578.6
4	Textiles and textile products	1,074.1	1,225.5	1,413.1	1,445.8	758.5	1,320.1	1,621.1	1,903.4	2,025.6	2,343.5
5	Leather, leather products, and footwear	207.3	247.1	281.7	285.8	146.9	281.1	375.5	441.9	463.7	460.5
6	Wood and products of wood and cork	606.0	650.1	718.2	724.1	396.5	770.3	865.6	988.1	958.3	896.4
7	Paper products, printing, and publishing	1,112.9	1,260.5	1,368.8	1,282.6	695.3	1,291.1	1,522.9	1,847.3	2,203.1	2,408.9
8	Coke, refined petroleum, and nuclear fuel	2,278.4	2,833.8	3,227.1	3,102.1	1,566.2	2,754.0	3,722.6	4,502.1	4,749.1	4,958.9
9	Chemicals and chemical products	1,514.0	1,690.5	2,108.4	2,107.0	1,169.9	2,359.0	2,839.2	3,363.1	3,420.5	3,699.7
10	Rubber and plastics	1,139.8	1,258.5	1,448.2	1,322.8	669.1	1,246.1	1,594.1	1,938.8	1,696.5	1,570.2
11	Other nonmetallic minerals	654.4	731.1	898.5	903.2	483.1	949.7	1,158.3	1,305.8	1,286.3	1,256.6
12	Basic metals and fabricated metal	1,449.9	1,665.7	1,953.3	2,047.8	1,078.1	2,040.4	2,411.4	2,982.0	3,188.1	3,212.7
13	Machinery, nec	439.7	442.7	509.9	478.1	299.0	581.8	674.9	792.6	950.5	909.2
14	Electrical and optical equipment	1,262.9	1,404.6	1,747.0	1,822.1	934.5	1,859.2	2,194.8	2,570.9	2,619.0	2,639.2
15	Transport equipment	1,248.3	1,474.0	1,717.0	1,816.0	941.9	1,800.4	2,225.2	2,602.4	2,603.0	2,511.4
16	Manufacturing, nec; recycling	407.4	444.6	493.9	487.0	265.7	512.8	626.8	740.4	706.4	757.3
17	Electricity, gas, and water supply	871.6	1,195.7	1,133.3	1,028.9	1,161.8	1,294.7	1,714.3	2,379.0	2,443.5	2,626.5
18	Construction	7,209.8	9,424.3	11,865.9	11,760.9	11,105.6	12,304.0	15,833.3	17,513.7	16,530.5	15,380.4
19	Sale and maintenance	5,217.6	5,938.0	6,589.8	6,713.2	6,418.9	6,862.9	8,628.4	9,226.5	9,474.8	9,755.8
20	Wholesale trade	13,447.9	15,405.8	16,582.2	16,432.4	15,625.4	16,531.7	21,212.3	23,108.1	23,947.8	24,336.6
21	Retail trade	7,889.2	9,043.9	9,734.5	9,646.6	9,191.8	9,740.5	12,452.8	13,565.7	14,087.5	14,316.2
22	Hotels and restaurants	5,983.3	6,847.0	8,562.1	9,562.1	9,682.6	7,979.4	10,125.4	13,319.9	15,088.6	16,354.3
23	Inland transport	4,988.4	5,359.7	2,747.4	2,528.7	1,838.5	3,748.0	5,245.5	5,392.8	5,464.6	5,926.7
24	Water transport	1,622.7	1,782.5	928.0	810.7	591.9	1,219.6	1,615.7	1,600.8	1,379.7	1,505.8
25	Air transport	2,046.4	2,473.4	1,557.5	1,500.8	1,285.4	2,698.8	3,729.4	4,350.5	5,340.7	5,606.0
26	Other transport services	1,195.4	1,354.8	747.6	691.4	528.7	1,132.3	1,685.4	1,810.0	1,650.8	1,890.4
27	Post and telecommunications	1,149.3	1,279.6	896.4	1,048.6	954.5	1,764.0	2,262.9	3,160.5	3,334.1	3,324.5
28	Financial intermediation	2,353.3	3,530.7	4,821.8	5,307.3	4,619.9	5,250.7	5,996.4	6,535.9	6,647.3	6,257.3
29	Real estate activities	258.3	387.5	600.6	666.8	799.3	845.4	1,228.2	904.9	1,015.3	1,224.7
30	Renting and other business activities	1,951.1	2,927.3	3,630.3	2,683.7	3,463.1	3,540.2	3,740.0	4,974.4	4,820.5	5,013.9
31	Public administration and defense	7,626.3	9,312.4	8,872.2	9,291.3	8,489.0	11,678.4	14,606.6	17,131.3	16,876.8	16,644.3
32	Education	10,461.3	12,774.2	17,231.4	17,054.1	16,305.8	12,349.7	14,054.7	15,271.7	15,176.9	14,710.2
33	Health and social work	2,544.9	3,107.6	3,278.8	3,293.7	3,230.4	4,153.3	4,299.9	5,316.5	5,627.5	5,616.1
34	Other services	10,453.7	12,765.0	8,356.0	8,135.5	8,050.2	5,760.4	6,451.4	7,963.0	8,242.7	8,673.7
35	Private households with employed persons	–	–	–	–	–	–	–	–	–	–

– = data not available, nec = not elsewhere classified.

Sources: ADB. Multi-Regional Input–Output Database. https://data.adb.org/taxonomy/term/476 (accessed 20 October 2021); and International Labour Organization. Indonesia Labour Force Surveys. https://www.ilo.org/dyn/lfsurvey/lfsurvey.list?p_lang=en&p_country=ID (accessed 20 October 2021).

Table A3.2: Employment in the Input–Output Table for Indonesia
(thousand)

		2010	2011	2012	2013	2014	2015	2016	2017	2018	2019
1	Agriculture, hunting, forestry, and fishing	42,160.4	40,902.1	40,628.8	39,992.5	39,904.3	38,936.6	38,034.9	37,804.2	37,201.8	36,343.5
2	Mining and quarrying	1,221.6	1,408.8	1,608.1	1,490.0	1,529.0	1,365.1	1,387.7	1,372.4	1,418.9	1,398.7
3	Food, beverages, and tobacco	4,126.7	4,363.0	4,878.6	4,814.9	2,777.2	5,346.6	5,275.5	5,819.3	6,184.8	6,417.6
4	Textiles and textile products	746.7	780.0	832.6	862.0	472.3	791.8	812.7	842.7	897.3	1,031.6
5	Leather, leather products, and footwear	144.1	157.2	166.0	170.4	91.4	168.6	188.2	195.6	205.4	202.7
6	Wood and products of wood and cork	421.3	413.8	423.2	431.7	246.9	462.1	434.0	437.5	424.5	394.6
7	Paper products, printing, and publishing	773.7	802.2	806.5	764.7	432.9	774.4	763.5	817.9	975.9	1,060.4
8	Coke, refined petroleum, and nuclear fuel	1,583.8	1,803.6	1,901.4	1,849.6	975.2	1,651.9	1,866.3	1,993.3	2,103.8	2,183.0
9	Chemicals and chemical products	1,052.4	1,076.0	1,242.2	1,256.2	728.4	1,414.9	1,423.4	1,489.0	1,515.2	1,628.6
10	Rubber and plastics	792.4	801.0	853.2	788.7	416.6	747.4	799.2	858.4	751.5	691.2
11	Other nonmetallic minerals	454.9	465.3	529.4	538.5	300.8	569.6	580.7	578.2	569.8	553.2
12	Basic metals and fabricated metal	1,007.9	1,060.1	1,150.8	1,221.0	671.3	1,223.8	1,209.0	1,320.3	1,412.3	1,414.2
13	Machinery, nec	305.7	281.8	300.4	285.0	186.2	349.0	338.3	350.9	421.0	400.2
14	Electrical and optical equipment	877.9	894.0	1,029.3	1,086.4	581.9	1,115.2	1,100.4	1,138.3	1,160.2	1,161.8
15	Transport equipment	867.8	938.1	1,011.7	1,082.7	586.5	1,079.9	1,115.6	1,152.0	1,153.1	1,105.5
16	Manufacturing, nec; recycling	283.2	283.0	291.0	290.4	165.5	307.6	314.2	327.8	312.9	333.3
17	Electricity, gas, and water supply	367.2	404.1	384.7	376.8	446.5	490.9	564.7	689.8	794.7	789.7
18	Construction	5,218.8	5,965.4	6,499.7	6,651.2	7,246.0	7,961.2	7,842.9	7,649.8	7,679.3	8,065.1
19	Sale and maintenance	3,584.3	3,718.7	4,164.1	4,337.7	4,407.5	4,547.3	4,662.0	4,595.8	4,648.7	4,864.0
20	Wholesale trade	9,238.3	9,647.8	10,478.4	10,617.6	10,729.1	10,953.8	11,461.3	11,510.3	11,749.6	12,133.7
21	Retail trade	5,419.6	5,663.7	6,151.3	6,233.1	6,311.5	6,454.0	6,728.4	6,757.2	6,911.8	7,137.7
22	Hotels and restaurants	4,110.3	4,287.9	3,932.1	4,504.1	4,824.3	5,166.9	5,942.5	6,993.4	7,879.1	8,626.6
23	Inland transport	2,592.7	2,332.9	2,134.2	2,144.7	2,024.3	1,969.2	2,069.2	2,049.9	2,072.2	2,137.2
24	Water transport	843.4	775.9	720.8	687.5	651.8	640.8	637.3	608.5	523.2	543.0
25	Air transport	1,063.6	1,076.6	1,209.8	1,272.9	1,415.3	1,417.9	1,471.1	1,653.7	2,025.2	2,021.5
26	Other transport services	621.3	589.7	580.7	586.4	582.2	594.9	664.8	688.0	626.0	681.7
27	Post and telecommunications	597.3	557.0	542.4	580.5	620.7	575.0	662.2	834.0	946.5	927.5
28	Financial intermediation	871.5	1,210.1	1,438.6	1,541.6	1,566.2	1,735.7	1,728.6	1,758.4	1,746.3	1,768.5
29	Real estate activities	95.6	132.8	189.0	207.8	256.9	292.2	335.1	319.2	329.2	369.2
30	Renting and other business activities	722.5	1,003.3	1,174.9	1,276.0	1,325.8	1,467.5	1,396.0	1,555.4	1,623.9	1,806.1
31	Public administration and defense	3,836.9	4,092.1	3,797.2	3,799.1	3,921.2	4,034.0	4,689.7	4,803.1	5,014.7	5,007.1
32	Education	5,263.2	5,613.3	5,257.3	5,380.5	5,621.6	5,748.7	5,911.4	6,184.6	6,188.5	6,455.9
33	Health and social work	1,280.4	1,365.6	1,286.2	1,356.3	1,409.7	1,505.5	1,698.6	1,812.7	1,931.0	1,968.1
34	Other services	5,259.4	5,609.2	5,676.3	5,867.2	5,921.9	5,824.4	5,470.3	5,818.8	6,138.2	6,317.5
35	Private households with employed persons	–	–	–	–	–	–	–	–	–	–

– = data not available, nec = not elsewhere classified.

Sources: ADB. Multi-Regional Input–Output Database. https://data.adb.org/taxonomy/term/476 (accessed 20 October 2021); and International Labour Organization. Indonesia Labour Force Surveys (accessed 20 October 2021).

Table A3.3: Summary of ADB Projects in Indonesia, 2010–2019
($ million)

A	Sovereign Loans/Programs	Approval	Construction/ Implementation Period	Total Finance	Financed by ADB	Target Direct Jobs
1	Infrastructure Reform Sector Development Program (Subprogram 3)	2010		300	200	N/A
2	Sixth Development Policy Support Program	2010		200	200	N/A
3	Low-Carbon and Resilient Development Program	2011		100	100	N/A
4	Precautionary Financing Facility	2012		500	500	N/A
5	Financial Market Development and Integration Program	2012		300	300	N/A
6	Inclusive Growth through Improved Connectivity Program (Subprogram 1)	2012		400	300	N/A
7	Inclusive Growth through Improved Connectivity Program (Subprogram 2)	2013		800	400	N/A
8	Sustainable and Inclusive Energy Program (Subprogram 1)	2015		900	400	N/A
9	Financial Market Development and Inclusion Program (Subprogram 1)	2015		400	400	N/A
10	Fiscal and Public Expenditure Management Program (Subprogram 1)	2016		724	500	N/A
11	Sustainable and Inclusive Energy Program (Subprogram 2)	2017		720	400	N/A
12	Financial Market Development and Inclusion Program (Subprogram 2)	2017		400	400	N/A
13	Fiscal and Public Expenditure Management Program (Subprogram 2)	2018		739	500	N/A
14	Stepping Up Investments for Growth Acceleration Program (Subprogram 3)	2018		840	500	N/A
15	Emergency Assistance for Recovery and Rehabilitation from Recent Disasters	2018		500	500	N/A
16	Financial Market Development and Inclusion Program (Subprogram 3)	2019		500	500	N/A
17	Fiscal and Public Expenditure Management Program (Subprogram 3)	2019		1,054	500	N/A
	Total			**9,377**	**6,600**	

B	Sovereign Loans/Projects	Approval	Construction/ Implementation Period	Total Finance	Financed by ADB	Target Direct Jobs
1	Java-Bali Electricity Distribution Performance Improvement Project	2010	2012–2015	101	50	N/A
2	Metropolitan Sanitation Management and Health Project	2010	2010–2020	64	35	N/A
3	Urban Sanitation and Rural Infrastructure Support to PNPM Mandiri Project	2011	2011–2016	100	100	N/A
4	Regional Roads Development Project	2011	2012–2019	381	180	N/A
5	Polytechnics Education Development Project	2012	2013–2019	92	75	N/A
6	State Accountability Revitalization Project	2012	2013–2020	61	58	N/A
7	West Kalimantan Power Grid Strengthening Project	2013	2013–2019	79	50	N/A
8	Java-Bali 500-Kilovolt Power Transmission Crossing	2013	2014–2020	385	224	N/A
9	Coral Reef Rehabilitation and Management Program-Coral Triangle Initiative Project	2013	2014–2022	59	46	N/A
10	Neighborhood Upgrading and Shelter Project (Phase 2)	2014	2014–2019	102	74	N/A
11	Metropolitan Sanitation Management Investment Project	2014	2014–2023	310	80	N/A
12	Electricity Grid Strengthening—Sumatra Program	2015	2016–2020	600	575	N/A
13	Flood Management in Selected River Basins Sector Project	2016	2016–2023	162	109	N/A
14	Accelerating Infrastructure Delivery through Better Engineering Services Project	2016	2016–2020	168	148	N/A
15	Integrated Participatory Development and Management of Irrigation Program	2017	2017–2023	1,551	500	N/A
16	Sustainable Energy Access in Eastern Indonesia-Electricity Grid Development Program	2017	2017–2022	1,830	600	N/A
17	Emergency Assistance for Rehabilitation and Reconstruction	2019		250	188	N/A
18	Advanced Knowledge and Skills for Sustainable Growth Project	2018	2019–2024	267	200	N/A
19	Leveraging Private Infrastructure Investment Project	2019	2019–2023	100	100	N/A
20	State Accountability Revitalization Project (Additional Financing)	2019	2020–2025	105	90	N/A
	Total			**6,763**	**3,481**	

continued on next page

Table A3.3 *continued*

C	Nonsovereign Loans	Approval	Construction/ Implementation Period	Total Finance	Financed by ADB	Target Direct Jobs
1	Indonesia: Loan to Indonesia Eximbank	2011	2010–2013	200	100	5,000
2	Sarulla Geothermal Power Generation Project	2013	2013–2017	1,239	330	1,624 construction, 100 operation
3	Rantau Dedap Geothermal Power Project (Phase 2)	2014	2014–2016	50	50	70 construction, 2 operation
4	Tangguh Liquefied Natural Gas Expansion Project	2016	2016–2018	400	400	7,000 construction, 29 operation
5	Muara Laboh Geothermal Power Project	2016	2017–2019	591	70	1,400 construction, 190 operation
6	Eastern Indonesia Renewable Energy Project (Phase 1)	2017	2017–2019	121	56	500 construction, 50 operation
7	Rantau Dedap Geothermal Power Project (Phase 2)	2018	2018–2020	710	178	1,000 construction, 100 operation
8	Maternity and Child Care Hospital Project	2018	2018–2020	180	10	4,281
9	Jawa-1 Liquefied Natural Gas-to-Power Project	2018	2018–2021	1,413	250	4,000 construction, 120 operation
	Total			**4,903**	**1,444**	**25,466**

ADB = Asian Development Bank.

Note: Numbers may not sum precisely because of rounding.

Source: ADB. Projects & Tenders. https://www.adb.org/projects (accessed 20 October 2021).

APPENDIX 4
Thailand

Table A4.1: Labor Compensation in the Input–Output Table for Thailand
($ million)

		2010	2011	2012	2013	2014	2015	2016	2017	2018	2019
1	Agriculture, hunting, forestry, and fishing	25,448.8	28,185.8	29,009.6	32,865.4	26,969.5	24,580.1	22,396.2	24,049.3	25,838.0	27,542.8
2	Mining and quarrying	168.4	246.4	490.7	417.2	609.4	508.9	384.4	360.0	404.2	368.1
3	Food, beverages, and tobacco	2,729.1	2,729.1	2,729.1	2,730.1	2,731.0	2,731.0	2,731.0	2,715.8	1,804.1	1,801.8
4	Textiles and textile products	682.8	682.8	682.8	682.6	682.5	682.5	682.5	644.9	843.6	842.5
5	Leather, leather products, and footwear	100.5	100.5	100.5	100.6	100.7	100.7	100.7	94.7	165.5	165.3
6	Wood and products of wood and cork	146.4	146.4	146.4	146.2	145.9	145.9	146.0	146.5	265.2	264.8
7	Paper products, printing, and publishing	309.9	309.8	309.8	309.3	308.8	308.8	308.8	304.7	830.6	849.9
8	Coke, refined petroleum, and nuclear fuel	1,182.0	1,182.0	1,182.0	1,189.0	1,195.9	1,196.1	1,195.7	1,382.9	111.1	110.9
9	Chemicals and chemical products	930.6	930.6	930.6	932.2	933.6	933.7	933.6	924.0	734.1	733.1
10	Rubber and plastics	958.1	958.1	958.1	957.7	957.3	957.3	957.4	979.6	1,788.1	1,785.8
11	Other nonmetallic minerals	782.9	782.9	782.9	784.0	785.0	785.0	785.0	746.9	320.9	320.5
12	Basic metals and fabricated metal	4,932.5	4,932.5	4,932.5	4,923.6	4,914.9	4,914.6	4,915.1	4,788.2	4,388.8	4,383.2
13	Machinery, nec	332.7	332.7	332.7	332.4	332.2	332.2	332.2	331.5	460.0	459.4
14	Electrical and optical equipment	406.6	406.6	406.6	406.5	406.5	406.5	406.5	375.4	440.6	440.0
15	Transport equipment	2,060.7	2,060.7	2,060.7	2,059.8	2,059.0	2,059.0	2,059.0	2,130.4	3,328.8	3,324.6
16	Manufacturing, nec; recycling	425.4	425.4	425.4	426.1	426.8	426.9	426.8	414.6	498.8	498.2
17	Electricity, gas, and water supply	888.4	1,439.2	1,307.9	1,459.6	1,684.8	1,373.1	1,655.0	1,773.8	1,561.4	1,830.4
18	Construction	5,215.3	6,102.1	7,083.4	8,204.2	7,751.8	7,595.2	7,768.1	7,417.1	7,932.8	8,609.6
19	Sale and maintenance	164.6	184.9	212.7	230.6	245.2	237.4	240.5	241.7	111.6	118.6
20	Wholesale trade	9,916.2	11,138.8	12,817.2	13,914.0	14,809.4	14,337.2	14,526.2	15,336.6	16,515.6	17,538.4
21	Retail trade	8,137.1	9,140.4	10,517.7	11,417.5	12,152.0	11,764.6	11,919.6	12,281.8	13,418.8	14,249.8
22	Hotels and restaurants	6,835.1	7,397.1	7,216.6	8,265.0	9,643.1	9,933.7	9,657.6	10,627.2	11,654.0	12,378.3
23	Inland transport	2,458.3	2,421.6	2,596.1	3,059.5	3,754.2	3,702.7	3,791.3	3,763.7	4,891.1	5,486.2
24	Water transport	676.2	666.1	714.1	842.1	1,033.9	1,019.8	1,044.2	1,061.5	750.9	842.3
25	Air transport	1,017.6	1,002.4	1,074.6	1,266.7	1,554.6	1,533.3	1,570.0	1,655.1	986.7	1,106.8
26	Other transport services	813.0	800.9	858.6	1,010.6	1,238.7	1,221.6	1,251.0	1,281.8	1,730.7	1,941.2
27	Post and telecommunications	1,474.0	1,607.0	2,003.3	1,907.3	2,462.3	2,136.5	2,197.1	2,095.6	1,925.8	2,321.2
28	Financial intermediation	3,153.0	3,414.8	3,675.7	4,269.7	5,115.3	4,528.5	4,629.4	4,490.8	4,569.8	5,099.8
29	Real estate activities	510.0	545.0	738.9	852.7	873.7	1,054.1	959.6	1,154.1	1,126.1	1,325.2
30	Renting and other business activities	2,956.3	3,267.5	3,470.3	3,854.3	4,745.2	5,397.3	5,209.7	5,526.7	6,180.3	6,377.9
31	Public administration and defense	7,831.6	8,383.0	9,484.9	9,684.3	9,522.8	9,464.0	9,162.4	9,790.8	10,860.5	11,266.1
32	Education	8,535.7	9,768.4	9,331.0	9,546.0	9,776.0	9,797.8	9,599.7	9,946.0	10,218.3	10,445.4
33	Health and social work	3,592.8	3,555.8	3,917.3	4,035.8	4,256.4	4,240.4	4,511.1	4,664.2	4,559.6	4,778.5
34	Other services	2,816.4	3,306.9	3,665.8	3,569.9	4,131.3	4,182.5	4,131.9	4,298.5	4,736.6	5,195.1
35	Private households with employed persons	–	–	–	–	–	–	–	–	–	–

– = data not available, nec = not elsewhere classified.

Note: Numbers may not sum precisely because of rounding.

Sources: ADB. Multi-Regional Input–Output Database. https://data.adb.org/taxonomy/term/476 (accessed 20 October 2021); and Thailand Labour Force Surveys. https://www.nso.go.th/sites/2014en/Pages/Statistical%20Themes/Population-Society/Labour/Labour-Force.aspx (accessed 20 October 2021).

Table A4.2: Employment in the Input–Output Table for Thailand
(thousand)

		2010	2011	2012	2013	2014	2015	2016	2017	2018	2019
1	Agriculture, hunting, forestry, and fishing	15,893.3	14,883.1	15,433.6	15,407.0	12,732.7	12,271.9	11,746.6	11,783.3	12,168.3	11,820.9
2	Mining and quarrying	34.9	50.0	72.9	65.9	69.0	79.2	66.5	64.5	73.5	60.7
3	Food, beverages, and tobacco	881.8	905.4	921.3	928.6	1,092.6	1,102.9	1,074.7	1,038.0	706.6	690.6
4	Textiles and textile products	220.6	226.5	230.5	232.2	273.1	275.6	268.6	246.5	330.4	322.9
5	Leather, leather products, and footwear	32.5	33.4	33.9	34.2	40.3	40.7	39.6	36.2	64.8	63.4
6	Wood and products of wood and cork	47.3	48.6	49.4	49.7	58.4	58.9	57.4	56.0	103.9	101.5
7	Paper products, printing, and publishing	100.1	102.8	104.6	105.2	123.5	124.7	121.5	116.5	325.3	325.7
8	Coke, refined petroleum, and nuclear fuel	381.9	392.1	399.0	404.4	478.5	483.0	470.5	528.5	43.5	42.5
9	Chemicals and chemical products	300.7	308.7	314.2	317.0	373.5	377.1	367.4	353.1	287.5	281.0
10	Rubber and plastics	309.6	317.8	323.4	325.7	383.0	386.6	376.7	374.4	700.3	684.5
11	Other nonmetallic minerals	253.0	259.7	264.3	266.7	314.1	317.0	308.9	285.5	125.7	122.8
12	Basic metals and fabricated metal	1,593.8	1,636.3	1,665.1	1,674.6	1,966.4	1,984.8	1,934.2	1,830.0	1,718.9	1,680.0
13	Machinery, nec	107.5	110.4	112.3	113.1	132.9	134.1	130.7	126.7	180.2	176.1
14	Electrical and optical equipment	131.4	134.9	137.2	138.3	162.6	164.2	160.0	143.5	172.5	168.6
15	Transport equipment	665.8	683.6	695.6	700.6	823.8	831.5	810.3	814.2	1,303.7	1,274.2
16	Manufacturing, nec; recycling	137.5	141.1	143.6	144.9	170.8	172.4	168.0	158.5	195.3	190.9
17	Electricity, gas, and water supply	115.1	190.1	161.2	187.6	222.5	187.9	217.2	226.1	190.4	215.6
18	Construction	2,010.3	2,371.9	2,493.1	2,542.6	2,269.2	2,281.8	2,352.1	2,160.2	2,112.4	2,191.2
19	Sale and maintenance	55.2	54.5	54.1	54.2	55.7	55.7	57.1	54.8	23.3	23.2
20	Wholesale trade	3,326.1	3,286.0	3,262.5	3,270.2	3,366.6	3,361.7	3,446.4	3,479.5	3,450.5	3,432.9
21	Retail trade	2,729.4	2,696.5	2,677.2	2,683.4	2,762.5	2,758.5	2,828.0	2,786.4	2,803.5	2,789.2
22	Hotels and restaurants	2,536.7	2,545.7	2,307.2	2,300.0	2,567.8	2,643.6	2,729.5	2,778.3	2,827.2	2,850.1
23	Inland transport	442.9	464.1	458.4	469.4	590.4	602.1	593.5	597.5	737.2	761.3
24	Water transport	121.8	127.7	126.1	129.2	162.6	165.8	163.4	168.5	113.2	116.9
25	Air transport	183.3	192.1	189.8	194.3	244.5	249.3	245.8	262.7	148.7	153.6
26	Other transport services	146.5	153.5	151.6	155.0	194.8	198.6	195.8	203.5	260.8	269.4
27	Post and telecommunications	173.1	181.4	213.8	199.2	248.0	241.8	231.3	219.7	199.0	196.3
28	Financial intermediation	373.3	395.5	417.8	440.5	526.8	539.2	545.6	524.5	500.8	515.5
29	Real estate activities	99.6	105.8	131.1	131.7	159.2	193.6	186.3	204.4	184.1	201.6
30	Renting and other business activities	623.6	662.5	627.5	651.2	812.0	921.0	933.9	950.3	946.8	981.5
31	Public administration and defense	1,521.7	1,596.4	1,713.6	1,640.0	1,589.4	1,611.2	1,579.4	1,588.8	1,626.5	1,611.4
32	Education	1,233.2	1,287.4	1,201.2	1,180.6	1,152.7	1,181.9	1,184.8	1,185.1	1,164.4	1,157.1
33	Health and social work	701.0	671.0	660.2	645.3	683.7	681.6	706.3	719.6	658.7	643.3
34	Other services	984.8	1,220.2	1,162.6	1,074.6	1,212.5	1,273.2	1,316.5	1,306.9	1,344.0	1,421.5
35	Private households with employed persons	–	–	–	–	–	–	–	–	–	–

– = data not available, nec = not elsewhere classified.

Note: Numbers may not sum precisely because of rounding.

Sources: ADB. Multi-Regional Input–Output Database. https://data.adb.org/taxonomy/term/476 (accessed 20 October 2021); and Thailand Labour Force Surveys. https://www.nso.go.th/sites/2014en/Pages/Statistical%20Themes/Population-Society/Labour/Labour-Force.aspx (accessed 20 October 2021).

Table A4.3: Summary of ADB Projects in Thailand, 2010–2019

A.	Nonsovereign Loans	Approval Year	Construction/ Implement Period	Total Finance	Financed by ADB	Estimated Direct Job creation	Reported Direct Job Creation[a]
1	Solar Power Project	2010	2010–2013	70.0	70.0	450 during construction and over 40 during operations	1,753 during construction, 882 during operations
2	Bangchak Solar Power Project	2010	2010–2011	145.0	145.0	200 jobs, 150 of which for local. 9 technical staffs for operation	200 during construction, 72 during operation
3	Nong Saeng Natural Gas Power Project	2011	2011–2014	1,462.0	170.0	1,200 people during construction and 70 permanent staff during operation, and purchasing $682 million in local goods during construction	3,873 during construction, 90 during operation
4	Provincial Solar Power Project	2012	2012–2013	37.6	12.6	100 people during construction. Over 80 commercial operations	Same
5	Ayudhaya Natural Gas Power Project	2012	2012–2015	1,516.2	185.0	4,569 people during the peak of construction, and an average of 1,915. Average of 70 permanent staff and 59 contract workers during operation	2,920 during construction, 154 during operation
6	Theppana Wind Power Project	2012	2012–2013	8.4	4.4	250 persons during construction and 13 staff during operations	Same
7	Central Thailand Solar Power Project	2013	2013–2014	88.7	35.0	150 people during construction and over 50 people during operations.	1,255 during construction, 66 during operation
8	Subyai Wind Power Project	2014	2014–2016	83.0	30.0	During construction, 250	419 during construction, 47 during operation
9	Distributed Commercial Solar Power Project	2016		125.4	47.0		
10	Grid-Parity Rooftop Solar Project	2016		116.2	43.6		
11	Southern Thailand Waste-to-Energy Project	2017	2017–2020	32.7	32.7	300 during construction, 65 employed in operations	136 during construction
12	Cornerstone Investment in Leading Independent Power Producer Project			120.0	45.0	Equity investment	212 during construction, 352 during operation
13	Bond Guarantee for Renewable Energy and Energy Storage Project	2017					
14	Bangkok Mass Rapid Transit Project (Pink and Yellow Lines)	2018	2018–2021	2,960.0	318.0	The 410 full-time staff and 160 temporary staff that the construction of the Yellow Line Project During the operation phase, around 230 workers will be employed in 23 stations. The 1,600 persons (1,400 workers and 200 staff) that the construction of the Pink Line Project During the operation phase, around 300 workers will be employed in 30 stations.	
15	Exacta Asia Investment II, L.P	2018		25.0	25.0	Equity	
16	Chonburi Natural Gas Power Project	2018	2018–2022	1151.0	228.0	3,200 during construction, 60 during operation	

continued on next page

Table A4.3   *continued*

A.	Nonsovereign Loans	Approval Year	Construction/ Implement Period	Total Finance	Financed by ADB	Estimated Direct Job creation	Reported Direct Job Creation[a]
17	Thailand Green Bond Project	2018	2018–2020	154.6	154.6	Approximately 200–300 during construction phases (approximately six-eight months). During operations, a solar farm can be maintained with a staff of approximately 10–15 workers	
18	Proposed Additional Capital Contribution Credit Guarantee and Investment Facility	2019		499.0	50.0		
19	Energy Absolute Green Bond for Wind Power Project	2019		325.1	97.4		
20	Kaizen Private Equity II Pte. Ltd.	2019		5.0	5.0	Equity	
21	Everbridge Partners Fund I, L.P.	2019		40.0	40.0	Equity	
22	Eastern Economic Corridor Independent Power Project	2019	2019–2024.	1152.0	50.0	3,200 jobs during construction, 60 during operation,	
23	Southern Thailand Wind Power and Battery Energy Storage Project	2019	2019–2020	12.3	4.8	694 during construction, 7 during operation	

B.	Sovereign Loans	Approval	Construction / Implement Period	Total Finance	Financed by ADB	Target Direct Jobs
24	Capital Market Development Program (CMDP)	2010		300.0	300.0	
25	Greater Mekong Subregion Highway Expansion Phase 2 Project	2017	2018–2022	213.6	99.4	917 workers, 399 locally hired

– = data not available, ADB = Asian Development Bank.

Note: Numbers may not sum precisely because of rounding.

[a] Data reported in *Development Effectiveness Monitoring Reports* and *Extended Annual Review Reports*.

Source: ADB. Projects & Tenders. https://www.adb.org/projects (accessed 20 October 2021).

Employment Multipliers, 2010-2019

Sector	2010 Thailand I	II	Indonesia I	II	Fiji I	II	2011 Thailand I	II	Indonesia I	II	Fiji I	II	2012 Thailand I	II	Indonesia I	II	Fiji I	II	2013 Thailand I	II	Indonesia I	II	Fiji I	II	2014 Thailand I	II	Indonesia I	II	Fiji I	II
1 Agriculture, hunting, forestry, and fishing	1.11	1.25	1.09	1.13	2.22	2.49	1.11	1.25	1.09	1.14	2.29	2.55	1.11	1.23	1.09	1.14	2.69	2.72	1.11	1.24	1.09	1.14	2.65	2.67	1.12	1.25	1.08	1.13	2.38	2.61
2 Mining and quarrying	13.47	16.79	2.19	2.44	1.65	1.93	8.99	11.10	2.17	2.42	1.54	1.72	6.20	7.78	2.03	2.26	1.63	1.65	6.82	8.58	2.07	2.32	1.47	1.48	6.99	8.98	1.95	2.14	1.40	1.48
3 Food, beverages, and tobacco	13.61	15.53	6.87	7.24	1.61	1.72	9.76	11.12	6.38	6.72	1.64	1.75	10.85	12.26	5.94	6.28	1.72	1.74	11.34	12.93	5.79	6.10	1.66	1.67	9.05	10.32	9.29	9.71	1.57	1.64
4 Textiles and textile products	3.51	4.29	2.77	2.97	1.53	1.61	2.82	3.39	2.60	2.78	1.55	1.64	2.96	3.53	2.49	2.68	1.61	1.62	3.01	3.61	2.46	2.63	1.57	1.59	2.85	3.38	3.39	3.59	1.48	1.54
5 Leather, leather products, and footwear	3.57	4.34	2.65	2.85	1.86	1.97	2.81	3.37	2.44	2.61	1.89	1.99	2.97	3.55	2.37	2.55	1.95	1.97	3.03	3.63	2.32	2.48	1.57	1.58	2.85	3.39	3.26	3.45	1.66	1.73
6 Wood and products of wood and cork	4.94	5.81	4.83	5.11	1.65	1.75	3.38	3.95	4.55	4.82	1.69	1.80	3.53	4.08	4.27	4.54	1.77	1.79	3.63	4.21	4.13	4.38	1.71	1.72	3.24	3.73	6.27	6.59	1.63	1.71
7 Paper products, printing, and publishing	2.93	3.58	3.05	3.28	1.41	1.49	2.12	2.54	2.94	3.16	1.42	1.50	2.21	2.63	2.84	3.06	1.49	1.50	2.23	2.67	2.81	3.01	1.40	1.41	2.12	2.52	3.87	4.11	1.29	1.34
8 Coke, refined petroleum, and nuclear fuel	3.39	4.16	1.64	1.78	1.00	1.05	1.85	2.22	1.59	1.72	1.34	1.41	2.02	2.42	1.55	1.69	1.04	1.05	2.08	2.49	1.53	1.66	1.04	1.04	2.08	2.47	2.00	2.15	1.00	1.00
9 Chemicals and chemical products	4.12	5.02	2.74	2.94	1.75	1.86	2.63	3.15	2.57	2.76	1.81	1.92	2.80	3.34	2.43	2.61	1.89	1.91	2.89	3.46	2.39	2.57	1.80	1.82	2.79	3.31	3.33	3.53	1.66	1.73
10 Rubber and plastics	5.69	6.70	4.90	5.19	1.45	1.53	3.83	4.47	4.51	4.78	1.46	1.54	3.99	4.62	4.11	4.37	1.52	1.54	4.19	4.88	4.04	4.29	1.44	1.45	3.73	4.33	6.21	6.52	1.31	1.37
11 Other nonmetallic minerals	3.61	4.47	2.22	2.40	1.66	1.79	2.06	2.49	2.12	2.29	1.77	1.89	2.24	2.69	2.02	2.19	1.91	1.92	2.30	2.78	2.01	2.17	1.87	1.89	2.28	2.74	2.77	2.96	1.92	2.01
12 Basic metals and fabricated metal	3.16	3.87	2.22	2.40	1.73	1.83	2.41	2.89	2.12	2.29	1.74	1.84	2.56	3.06	2.02	2.19	1.81	1.83	2.63	3.14	2.01	2.17	1.70	1.71	2.59	3.07	2.74	2.93	1.57	1.64
13 Machinery, nec	3.38	4.15	2.25	2.43	1.28	1.36	2.46	2.96	2.16	2.33	1.29	1.36	2.62	3.14	2.06	2.22	1.35	1.36	2.66	3.21	2.07	2.22	1.29	1.30	2.57	3.07	2.73	2.90	1.16	1.21
14 Electrical and optical equipment	3.28	4.05	2.53	2.73	1.00	1.05	2.57	3.11	2.47	2.66	1.04	1.04	2.73	3.29	2.39	2.57	1.04	1.05	2.78	3.37	2.37	2.54	1.04	1.04	2.67	3.22	3.21	3.42	1.03	1.07
15 Transport equipment	3.07	3.76	2.39	2.58	1.44	1.52	2.19	2.63	2.34	2.52	1.45	1.53	2.30	2.73	2.24	2.42	1.52	1.53	2.33	2.78	2.23	2.40	1.40	1.41	2.29	2.69	3.07	3.27	1.30	1.35
16 Manufacturing, nec; recycling	4.17	5.04	3.01	3.23	1.82	1.92	2.96	3.52	2.87	3.08	1.85	1.95	3.13	3.71	2.73	2.94	1.92	1.94	3.22	3.83	2.70	2.90	1.84	1.85	2.99	3.54	3.81	4.04	1.75	1.82
17 Electricity, gas, and water supply	5.76	7.54	4.00	4.43	1.41	1.53	2.83	3.76	3.96	4.41	1.44	1.54	3.00	3.96	4.03	4.48	1.51	1.53	2.95	3.89	3.92	4.33	1.42	1.43	2.94	3.88	3.60	3.94	1.55	1.63
18 Construction	1.50	1.81	3.03	3.25	1.46	1.37	1.25	1.46	2.76	2.96	1.39	1.48	1.24	1.45	2.66	2.87	1.46	1.48	1.23	1.46	2.66	2.86	1.51	1.52	1.28	1.53	2.46	2.61	1.28	1.31
19 Sale and maintenance	1.49	1.83	1.19	1.28	1.15	1.21	1.41	1.72	1.19	1.28	1.15	1.21	1.41	1.73	1.26	1.26	1.20	1.21	1.41	1.75	1.18	1.26	1.04	1.05	1.43	1.79	1.17	1.24	1.25	1.30
20 Wholesale trade	1.28	1.56	1.19	1.28	1.20	1.27	1.21	1.47	1.18	1.27	1.20	1.27	1.21	1.48	1.17	1.26	1.26	1.27	1.21	1.50	1.17	1.25	1.87	1.89	1.22	1.52	1.16	1.24	1.18	1.23
21 Retail trade	1.31	1.60	1.19	1.28	1.16	1.22	1.24	1.51	1.18	1.27	1.16	1.22	1.24	1.52	1.17	1.26	1.22	1.23	1.24	1.54	1.17	1.26	1.20	1.21	1.25	1.56	1.17	1.24	1.19	1.24
22 Hotels and restaurants	1.93	2.26	2.34	2.49	1.32	1.40	1.82	2.12	2.24	2.38	1.35	1.44	1.92	2.24	2.41	2.60	1.44	1.45	2.02	2.37	2.27	2.43	1.42	1.43	1.89	2.25	2.13	2.26	1.40	1.48
23 Inland transport	2.23	2.91	1.40	1.54	1.58	1.72	1.83	2.33	1.41	1.55	1.61	1.75	1.81	2.31	1.46	1.55	1.78	1.80	1.81	2.36	1.50	1.59	1.77	1.78	1.71	2.23	1.53	1.60	1.03	1.13
24 Water transport	2.13	2.81	1.61	1.76	1.82	1.97	1.84	2.35	1.62	1.78	1.87	2.03	1.85	2.42	1.68	1.80	2.07	2.09	1.86	2.42	1.75	1.86	1.85	1.86	1.77	2.31	1.80	1.89	1.33	1.45
25 Air transport	2.55	3.35	1.54	1.69	1.80	1.96	2.20	2.81	1.57	1.72	1.87	2.03	2.22	2.84	1.62	1.73	2.08	2.10	2.23	2.91	1.72	1.82	1.89	1.91	2.09	2.73	1.80	1.88	1.35	1.47
26 Other transport services	2.38	3.12	1.47	1.61	1.67	1.83	1.90	2.44	1.49	1.65	1.72	1.88	1.89	2.43	1.54	1.65	1.92	1.93	1.89	2.48	1.59	1.69	1.90	1.92	1.80	2.36	1.65	1.73	1.23	1.34
27 Post and telecommunications	2.41	3.41	2.26	2.48	1.62	1.82	2.08	2.91	2.37	2.60	1.61	1.78	1.99	2.79	2.46	2.67	1.69	1.70	2.15	3.01	2.40	2.60	1.63	1.64	2.09	2.97	2.29	2.45	1.29	1.37
28 Financial intermediation	1.85	2.68	1.92	2.15	1.60	1.81	1.72	2.43	1.70	1.91	1.58	1.78	1.71	2.38	1.67	1.89	1.80	1.82	1.75	2.49	1.67	1.88	1.78	1.79	1.75	2.50	1.64	1.81	1.40	1.53
29 Real estate activities	2.81	3.67	4.71	5.17	2.15	2.26	2.51	3.22	3.73	4.10	2.10	2.21	2.12	2.74	2.96	3.28	2.21	2.23	2.10	2.77	2.83	3.13	2.08	2.09	1.96	2.54	2.46	2.69	3.78	4.00
30 Renting and other business activities	3.15	3.99	2.11	2.35	1.15	1.22	2.44	3.06	1.83	2.04	1.13	1.20	2.65	3.32	1.75	1.96	1.19	1.20	2.57	3.26	1.73	1.88	1.18	1.18	2.34	2.99	1.71	1.86	1.34	1.41
31 Public administration and defense	1.38	1.82	1.44	1.58	1.08	1.19	1.31	1.69	1.43	1.56	1.11	1.22	1.27	1.64	1.48	1.63	1.18	1.19	1.29	1.69	1.50	1.65	1.16	1.17	1.33	1.74	1.48	1.60	1.11	1.21
32 Education	1.48	2.07	1.21	1.33	1.05	1.16	1.37	1.90	1.20	1.33	1.08	1.19	1.39	1.90	1.24	1.41	1.15	1.15	1.42	1.96	1.24	1.41	1.13	1.14	1.46	2.02	1.21	1.35	1.11	1.21
33 Health and social work	1.66	2.15	2.01	2.18	1.07	1.16	1.62	2.05	1.95	2.12	1.09	1.18	1.59	2.03	2.05	2.24	1.14	1.15	1.68	2.15	2.01	2.19	1.12	1.13	1.69	2.16	1.94	2.09	1.09	1.17
34 Other services	1.26	1.53	1.50	1.66	1.19	1.32	1.17	1.37	1.49	1.65	1.19	1.31	1.19	1.40	1.49	1.60	1.28	1.29	1.21	1.44	1.50	1.60	1.24	1.25	1.20	1.44	1.52	1.60	1.04	1.08
35 Private households with employed persons	–	–	–	–	–	–	–	–	–	–	–	–	–	–	–	–	–	–	–	–	–	–	–	–	–	–	–	–	–	–

continued on next page

Appendix 5 *continued*

Sector	2015 Thailand I	Thailand II	Indonesia I	Indonesia II	Fiji I	Fiji II	2016 Thailand I	Thailand II	Indonesia I	Indonesia II	Fiji I	Fiji II	2017 Thailand I	Thailand II	Indonesia I	Indonesia II	Fiji I	Fiji II	2018 Thailand I	Thailand II	Indonesia I	Indonesia II	Fiji I	Fiji II	2019 Thailand I	Thailand II	Indonesia I	Indonesia II	Fiji I	Fiji II
1 Agriculture, hunting, forestry, and fishing	1.11	1.24	1.08	1.13	1.64	1.77	1.10	1.22	1.10	1.15	1.66	1.80	1.10	1.17	1.09	1.14	1.71	1.87	1.12	1.19	1.09	1.17	1.51	1.64	1.11	1.18	1.09	1.16	1.53	1.65
2 Mining and quarrying	5.70	7.24	2.02	2.21	1.55	1.67	6.05	7.47	1.93	2.14	1.54	1.65	5.82	6.63	2.03	2.27	1.56	1.68	5.17	5.92	2.14	2.47	1.42	1.50	6.07	6.95	2.12	2.41	1.39	1.46
3 Food, beverages, and tobacco	9.23	10.52	5.59	5.86	1.71	1.81	9.22	10.37	5.09	5.39	1.75	1.85	9.24	9.95	4.67	4.98	1.61	1.70	9.38	10.12	4.83	5.24	1.48	1.55	8.86	9.56	4.73	5.10	1.48	1.54
4 Textiles and textile products	2.89	3.44	2.49	2.64	1.47	1.55	3.00	3.52	2.69	2.89	1.53	1.61	2.94	3.25	2.31	2.51	1.44	1.51	3.07	3.41	1.14	1.27	1.31	1.35	2.97	3.28	1.35	1.49	1.32	1.37
5 Leather, leather products, and footwear	2.89	3.45	2.49	2.65	1.74	1.83	2.99	3.51	2.71	2.92	1.76	1.84	2.92	3.23	2.21	2.40	1.63	1.70	3.05	3.39	1.15	1.29	1.45	1.50	3.23	3.51	1.39	1.54	1.46	1.51
6 Wood and products of wood and cork	3.28	3.79	4.22	4.45	1.78	1.88	3.29	3.76	3.95	4.21	1.82	1.92	3.28	3.56	3.66	3.93	1.68	1.76	3.24	3.52	3.68	3.91	1.56	1.63	3.51	3.83	3.53	3.83	1.55	1.62
7 Paper products, printing, and publishing	2.16	2.57	2.90	3.09	1.33	1.41	2.21	2.59	2.94	3.18	1.34	1.41	2.18	2.40	2.70	2.95	1.28	1.34	2.24	2.48	2.67	2.98	1.13	1.18	2.16	2.38	2.70	2.98	1.13	1.17
8 Coke, refined petroleum, and nuclear fuel	2.25	2.67	1.74	1.87	1.00	1.00	2.40	2.81	1.60	1.74	1.00	1.00	2.25	2.47	1.77	1.95	1.00	1.00	2.43	2.67	1.60	1.80	1.00	1.00	2.41	2.65	1.64	1.83	1.00	1.00
9 Chemicals and chemical products	2.91	3.46	2.63	2.80	1.74	1.84	3.06	3.58	2.68	2.88	1.78	1.88	2.97	3.27	2.42	2.63	1.65	1.74	3.20	3.54	2.40	2.67	1.49	1.56	3.11	3.43	2.47	2.72	1.48	1.54
10 Rubber and plastics	3.76	4.37	4.18	4.40	1.37	1.45	3.80	4.36	4.16	4.43	1.40	1.47	3.80	4.13	3.98	4.27	1.32	1.39	3.93	4.29	3.39	3.72	1.13	1.17	3.83	4.17	3.45	3.75	1.11	1.15
11 Other nonmetallic minerals	2.46	2.96	2.30	2.46	1.88	2.00	2.64	3.13	2.20	2.38	1.94	2.06	2.49	2.77	2.15	2.36	1.81	1.91	2.67	2.97	2.06	2.31	1.40	1.46	2.64	2.93	2.13	2.36	1.39	1.45
12 Basic metals and fabricated metal	2.73	3.24	2.26	2.42	1.64	1.73	2.87	3.36	2.25	2.44	1.67	1.76	2.74	3.02	2.16	2.36	1.58	1.65	2.82	3.11	2.06	2.31	1.40	1.45	2.80	3.08	2.14	2.37	1.38	1.43
13 Machinery, nec	2.66	3.19	2.32	2.47	1.19	1.25	2.79	3.29	3.00	3.25	1.21	1.27	2.69	2.98	2.23	2.43	1.16	1.22	2.88	3.20	2.34	2.62	1.11	1.15	2.71	3.01	2.48	2.74	1.11	1.15
14 Electrical and optical equipment	2.78	3.35	2.57	2.74	1.04	1.09	2.91	3.45	3.03	3.28	1.02	1.07	2.81	3.13	2.42	2.65	1.38	1.44	2.97	3.31	2.25	2.52	1.00	1.00	2.86	3.18	2.38	2.63	1.00	1.00
15 Transport equipment	2.37	2.80	2.40	2.55	1.32	1.38	2.46	2.87	2.50	2.71	1.37	1.44	2.37	2.61	2.26	2.47	1.30	1.36	2.37	2.60	2.15	2.41	1.10	1.14	2.37	2.60	2.21	2.44	1.10	1.14
16 Manufacturing, nec; recycling	3.07	3.64	2.80	2.97	1.81	1.90	3.16	3.70	2.87	3.09	1.84	1.94	3.09	3.40	2.62	2.85	1.72	1.80	3.22	3.55	2.48	2.77	1.60	1.66	3.09	3.40	2.53	2.79	1.61	1.67
17 Electricity, gas, and water supply	3.53	4.62	3.95	4.30	1.45	1.53	3.30	4.23	3.82	4.24	1.45	1.53	2.94	3.45	3.42	3.85	1.44	1.52	3.77	4.41	2.81	3.23	1.38	1.46	3.68	4.30	2.97	3.38	1.40	1.48
18 Construction	1.33	1.59	2.72	2.89	1.33	1.38	1.34	1.58	2.82	3.05	1.33	1.37	1.32	1.46	2.68	2.92	1.31	1.35	1.35	1.50	3.22	3.58	1.24	1.28	1.34	1.49	3.27	3.59	1.22	1.25
19 Sale and maintenance	1.46	1.83	1.20	1.28	1.21	1.25	1.53	1.88	1.20	1.29	1.16	1.21	1.52	1.73	1.18	1.28	1.23	1.23	1.58	1.81	1.17	1.30	1.15	1.20	1.63	1.86	1.17	1.29	1.15	1.20
20 Wholesale trade	1.24	1.55	1.19	1.26	1.14	1.19	1.27	1.55	1.19	1.28	1.14	1.19	1.27	1.44	1.18	1.28	1.17	1.20	1.29	1.47	1.16	1.29	1.14	1.18	1.32	1.51	1.17	1.28	1.14	1.18
21 Retail trade	1.28	1.59	1.19	1.26	1.12	1.18	1.31	1.60	1.19	1.28	1.13	1.18	1.31	1.48	1.18	1.28	1.15	1.19	1.34	1.53	1.16	1.29	1.12	1.16	1.37	1.56	1.17	1.28	1.12	1.16
22 Hotels and restaurants	1.93	2.30	2.17	2.28	1.38	1.46	2.74	3.17	1.95	2.07	1.37	1.45	2.78	3.05	1.76	1.88	1.36	1.44	3.01	3.31	1.76	1.99	1.35	1.41	3.06	3.38	1.57	1.70	1.36	1.43
23 Inland transport	1.75	2.28	1.59	1.71	1.06	1.16	1.56	2.01	1.58	1.73	1.08	1.17	1.55	1.81	1.58	1.74	1.05	1.15	1.57	1.84	1.77	2.01	1.02	1.10	1.58	1.86	1.85	2.07	1.01	1.08
24 Water transport	1.83	2.38	1.98	2.12	1.27	1.39	1.65	2.12	1.99	2.18	1.27	1.38	1.61	1.88	1.95	2.15	1.23	1.34	1.67	1.96	1.95	2.21	1.25	1.34	1.67	1.97	2.04	2.28	1.21	1.30
25 Air transport	2.15	2.79	1.89	2.03	1.31	1.42	1.91	2.46	1.76	1.92	1.30	1.41	1.89	2.20	1.77	1.96	1.26	1.37	1.92	2.26	2.13	2.41	1.16	1.25	1.94	2.28	2.22	2.48	1.12	1.20
26 Other transport services	1.86	2.44	1.67	1.80	1.14	1.25	1.67	2.16	1.67	1.84	1.14	1.24	1.65	1.93	1.65	1.83	1.11	1.21	1.66	1.96	1.76	1.99	1.14	1.23	1.66	1.96	1.80	2.02	1.15	1.22
27 Post and telecommunications	2.34	3.24	2.51	2.75	1.38	1.51	2.08	2.86	2.21	2.47	1.39	1.52	2.11	2.56	2.00	2.26	1.38	1.50	2.28	2.77	2.29	2.77	1.30	1.40	2.38	2.94	2.40	2.66	1.34	1.44
28 Financial intermediation	1.80	2.50	1.62	1.79	1.48	1.66	1.83	2.47	1.41	1.59	1.47	1.64	1.83	2.21	1.40	1.60	1.46	1.63	1.90	2.32	1.62	1.91	1.39	1.54	1.89	2.30	1.66	1.90	1.40	1.53
29 Real estate activities	1.81	2.36	2.41	2.63	3.32	3.56	1.91	2.41	1.85	2.07	3.29	3.52	1.81	2.11	1.85	2.05	3.23	3.46	1.95	2.29	2.20	2.51	2.80	2.96	1.89	2.22	2.14	2.42	2.85	3.01
30 Renting and other business activities	2.20	2.82	1.72	1.87	1.30	1.38	2.29	2.85	1.71	1.88	1.30	1.38	2.20	2.52	1.63	1.82	1.30	1.38	2.28	2.64	1.72	1.97	1.28	1.34	2.26	2.61	1.73	1.94	1.28	1.35
31 Public administration and defense	1.35	1.76	1.51	1.66	1.11	1.25	1.36	1.74	1.44	1.60	1.11	1.23	1.35	1.57	1.40	1.58	1.10	1.24	1.35	1.59	1.44	1.67	1.06	1.17	1.36	1.59	1.46	1.66	1.06	1.18
32 Education	1.47	2.04	1.25	1.35	1.15	1.29	1.47	1.98	1.22	1.33	1.15	1.29	1.44	1.74	1.19	1.31	1.15	1.30	1.46	1.78	1.22	1.37	1.13	1.25	1.47	1.78	1.23	1.36	1.13	1.25
33 Health and social work	1.74	2.24	1.99	2.16	1.08	1.16	1.66	2.11	1.82	1.98	1.07	1.14	1.63	1.89	1.73	1.91	1.09	1.17	1.72	2.01	1.76	2.00	1.05	1.11	1.79	2.08	1.80	2.01	1.05	1.12
34 Other services	1.20	1.44	1.51	1.58	1.05	1.11	1.22	1.43	1.49	1.57	1.05	1.12	1.22	1.34	1.47	1.56	1.04	1.11	1.22	1.36	1.54	1.66	1.06	1.11	1.22	1.35	1.56	1.67	1.06	1.11
35 Private households with employed persons	–	–	–	–	–	–	–	–	–	–	–	–	–	–	–	–	–	–	–	–	–	–	–	–	–	–	–	–	–	–

– = data not available, nec = not elsewhere classified.

Source: ADB. Multi-Regional Input–Output Database. https://data.adb.org/taxonomy/term/476 (accessed 20 October 2021).

References

Aguiar, Angel, Maksym Chepeliev, Erwin Corong, Robert A. McDougall, and Dominique van der Mensbrugghe. 2019. "The GTAP Data Base: Version 10." *Journal of Global Economic Analysis* 4 (1): 1-27.

Anker, Richard, Igor Chernyshev, Philippe Egger, Farhad Mehran, and Joseph Ritter. 2002. "Measuring Decent Work with Statistical Indicators." Working Paper No. 2. International Labour Organization, Geneva.

Asian Development Bank (ADB). 2013a. *Cost–Benefit Analysis for Development: A Practical Guide.* Manila: Asian Development Bank.

———. 2013b. *Guidelines for the Use of ADB's Results Framework Indicators for Core Sector Outputs and Outcomes.* Manila: Asian Development Bank.

———. 2016. Policy-Based Lending. *Operations Manual.* Manila: Asian Development Bank.

———. 2018a. *Strategy 2030: Achieving a Prosperous, Inclusive, Resilient, and Sustainable Asia and the Pacific.* Manila: Asian Development Bank.

———. 2018b. *Policy-Based Lending 2008–2017: Performance, Results, and Issues of Design.* Manila: Asian Development Bank.

———. 2019. *ADB Corporate Results Framework, 2019–2024: Policy Paper.* Manila: Asian Development Bank.

———. 2020a. *2019 Development Effectiveness Review.* Manila: Asian Development Bank.

———. 2020b. *ADB's Comprehensive Response to the COVID-19 Pandemic: Policy Paper.* Manila: Asian Development Bank.

———. 2020c. *Guidelines for Preparing a Design and Monitoring Framework.* Manila: Asian Development Bank.

———. 2020d. *Key Indicators for Asia and the Pacific 2020.* Manila: Asian Development Bank.

———. 2021. *2020 Development Effectiveness Review.* Manila: Asian Development Bank.

———. 2022. *2021 Development Effectiveness Review.* Manila: Asian Development Bank.

Asquith, Joanne. 2017. "Corporate Evaluation of ADB Policy Based Lending." Evaluation Approach Paper. Manila: Asian Development Bank.

Bacon, Robert and Masami Kojima. 2011. *Issues in Estimating the Employment Generated by Energy Sector Activities.* Washington, DC: World Bank.

Bess, Rebecca and Zoë O. Ambargis. 2011. "Input–output Models for Impact Analysis: Suggestions for Practitioners Using RIMS II Multipliers." Paper presented at the 50th Southern Regional Science Association Conference, New Orleans.

Bourmpoula Evangelia, Roger Gomis, and Steven Kapsos. 2017. "ILO Labour Force Estimates and Projections: 1990–2030." Methodological Description. International Labour Office, Geneva.

Corong, Erwin, Thomas W. Hertel, Robert A. McDougall, Marinos E. Tsigas, and Dominique van der Mensbrugghe. 2017. "The Standard GTAP Model, Version 7." *Journal of Global Economic Analysis* 2 (1): 1-119.

Dixon, Peter B., B. R. Parmenter, John Sutton, and D. P. Vincent. 1982. *ORANI: A Multisectoral Model of the Australian Economy.* Amsterdam: North-Holland.

EORA Global Supply Chain Database. https://www.worldmrio.com/ (accessed 26 September 2022).

Faturay, Futu, Manfred Lenzen, and Kunta Nugraha. 2017. "A New Sub-national Multi-region Input–Output Database for Indonesia." *Economic Systems Research* 29 (2): 234–251.

Fiji Bureau of Statistics. 2019 and 2020. "Annual Paid Employment Statistics 2017 and 2018." Release No. 40. Suva. https://www.statsfiji.gov.fj/statistics/social-statistics/employment-statistics44.html (accessed 26 September 2022).

———. 2018. "Fiji's Gross Domestic Product 2017 Income Approach at Current Price." Release No. 76. Suva.

GTAP 10: Global Trade Analysis Project. https://www.gtap.agecon.purdue.edu/databases/utilities/v10.aspx (accessed 20 October 2021).

Horridge, Mark. 2000. "ORANI-G: A General Equilibrium Model of the Australian Economy." CoPS/IMPACT Working Paper Number OP-93. Victoria University, Melbourne. http://www.copsmodels.com/elecpapr/op-93.htm (accessed 20 December 2020).

Horridge, Mark, Arief Anshory Yusuf, Edimon Ginting, Priasto Aji. 2016. "Improving Indonesia's Domestic Connectivity: An Inter-regional CGE Analysis." ADB Papers on Indonesia No 17. Manila: Asian Development Bank.

ILOSTAT. 2020. ILOSTAT Database. International Labour Organization. https://ilostat.ilo.org/data/ (accessed 12 November 2021).

International Development Association (IDA). 2019. "IDA 19 Special Theme: Jobs and Economic Transformation." World Bank, Washington, DC.

International Finance Corporation (IFC). 2013. *IFC Jobs Study: Assessing Private Sector Contributions to Job Creation and Poverty Reduction.* Washington, DC: World Bank.

International Labour Organization (ILO). 2020. *Guide for Monitoring Employment and Conducting Employment Impact Assessment (EmpIA) of Infrastructure Investments.* Geneva.

Kluve, Jochen and Jonathan Stöterau. 2014. *A Systematic Framework for Measuring Employment Impacts of Development Cooperation Interventions.* Bonn: Deutsche Gesellschaft für Internationale Zusammenarbeit (GIZ) GmbH.

Kwangmoon, Kim, Francisco Secretario, Bui Trinh, and Hidefumi Kaneko. 2011. "Developing a Bilateral Input–output Table in the Case of Thailand and Vietnam: Methodology and Applications." 19th International Input–output Conference Proceedings, Alexandria, United States.

Leontief, Wassily. 1986. *Input–Output Economics.* Second Edition. New York, NY: Oxford University Press.

MacGillivray Alex and Aneese Lelijveld. 2019. *Measuring the Indirect Impact of Businesses in an Investment Portfolio: A Job Estimation Tool.* London: CDC Group.

Oum, Sothea and Rup Singh. 2019. "A New Computable General Equilibrium Model for the Fiji Economy." School of Economics Working Paper No. 2. The University of the South Pacific, Suva.

Papong, Seksan, Norihiro Itsubo, Pomthong Malakul, and Masanori Shukuya. 2015. "Development of the Social Inventory Database in Thailand Using Input–output Analysis." *Sustainability* 7 (6): 7684-7713.

Scottish Government. 2022. Supply, Use and Input-Output Tables. 26 October. https://www.gov.scot/publications/about-supply-use-input-output-tables/pages/user-guide-introduction/.

Steward Redqueen. 2021. Joint Impact Model: Methodology paper. https://jointimpactmodel.com/doc/JIM_Methodology.pdf (accessed 26 September 2022).

United Nations Statistics Division. 1999. *Handbook of Input–Output Table Compilation and Analysis.* New York, NY: United Nations. https://digitallibrary.un.org/record/370160?ln=en.

White, Howard and Raitzer, David A. 2017. *Impact Evaluation of Development Interventions: A Practical Guide.* Manila: Asian Development Bank.

Woltjer, Pieter, Reitze Gouma, and Marcel P. Timmer. 2021. World Input–output Database, 2021 Release, 1965–2000, Long-run WIOD. https://doi.org/10.34894/A7AXDN, DataverseNL, V2 (accessed 26 September 2022).

World Bank. 2012. *World Development Report 2013: Jobs.* Washington, DC: World Bank.

———. 2020. World Development Indicators. https://datatopics.worldbank.org/world-development-indicators/ (accessed 8 August 2020).

Woltjer, Pieter, Reitze Gouma, and Marcel P. Timmer. 2021. World Input–output Database, 2021 Release, 1965–2000, Long-run WIOD. https://doi.org/10.34894/A7AXDN, DataverseNL, V2 (accessed 26 September 2022).

www.ingramcontent.com/pod-product-compliance
Lightning Source LLC
Chambersburg PA
CBHW061221270326
41926CB00032B/4808